Take a Swing at Your Word Knowledge

The chips are down, saved by the bell, out in left field, hit and run. Sports idioms and metaphors are perfect for conveying the drama or the daffiness of life. Baseball alone has given us **southpaw, go to bat, coming out of left field,** and **hardball.** This fascinating collection reveals the roots and meanings of hundreds of phrases from the world of sports and games. Only an **oddball** who doesn't **know the score** would stay **on the sidelines** or **take a raincheck.**

> "Here's one for good sports. . . . All you need to do is take a quick skim through . . . and you might just be the 'big hitter' (important person) at the next party."
> —Calgary Sun

> "Delightful! The inside knowledge of the game, the dugouts, the technical details will open the eyes of many a smug maven."
> —LEO ROSTEN, author of The Joys of Yinglish

SOUTHPAWS AND SUNDAY PUNCHES

CHRISTINE AMMER, a lexicographer, is the author of fifteen books, including *Have a Nice Day—No Problem! A Dictionary of Cliches* and *Seeing Red or Tickled Pink*, as well as *Fighting Words* and *It's Raining Cats and Dogs and Other Beastly Expressions*. She lives in Lexington, Massachusetts.

OTHER BOOKS BY CHRISTINE AMMER

Seeing Red or Tickled Pink: Color Terms in Everyday Language
Have a Nice Day—No Problem! A Dictionary of Clichés
It's Raining Cats and Dogs and Other Beastly Expressions
Fighting Words from War, Rebellion and Other Combative Capers
Getting Help: A Consumer's Guide to Therapy
The New A to Z of Women's Health
The HarperCollins Dictionary of Music
Unsung: A History of Women in American Music
The A to Z of Investing

CHRISTINE AMMER

SOUTHPAWS

&

SUNDAY

PUNCHES

AND OTHER SPORTING EXPRESSIONS

A PLUME BOOK

PLUME

Published by the Penguin Group

Penguin Books USA Inc., 375 Hudson Street, New York, New York 10014, U.S.A.

Penguin Books Ltd, 27 Wrights Lane, London W8 5TZ, England

Penguin Books Australia Ltd, Ringwood, Victoria, Australia

Penguin Books Canada Ltd, 10 Alcorn Avenue, Toronto, Ontario, Canada M4V 3B2

Penguin Books (N.Z.) Ltd, 182–190 Wairau Road, Auckland 10, New Zealand

Penguin Books Ltd, Registered Offices:
Harmondsworth, Middlesex, England

Published by Plume, an imprint of Dutton Signet,
a division of Penguin Books USA Inc.
Previously published in a Dutton edition.

First Plume Printing, December, 1994

1 3 5 7 9 10 8 6 4 2

 REGISTERED TRADEMARK—MARCA REGISTRADA

The Library of Congress has cataloged the hardcover as follows:

LIBRARY OF CONGRESS CATALOGING-IN-PUBLICATION DATA

Ammer, Christine.
    Southpaws and sunday punches : and other sporting expressions / Christine
Ammer.
    p. cm.
    ISBN 0-525-93647-5 (hc.)
    ISBN 0-452-27248-3 (pbk.)
    1. English language—Terms and phrases. 2. English language—Etymology—
Dictionaries. 3. English language—Idioms—Dictionaries. 4. English language—
Figures of speech. 5. Sports—Terminology—Dictionaries. I. Title.
PE1689.A495 1993
422'.03—dc20   93-30801
                                                                                    CIP

Printed in the United States of America

Original hardcover design by Steven N. Stathakis

BOOKS ARE AVAILABLE AT QUANTITY DISCOUNTS WHEN USED TO PROMOTE PRODUCTS OR
SERVICES. FOR INFORMATION PLEASE WRITE TO PREMIUM MARKETING DIVISION,
PENGUIN BOOKS USA INC., 375 HUDSON STREET, NEW YORK, NEW YORK 10014.

For John and Dave

PREFACE

The box score's in, but don't jump the gun and leave our white hope out of the money. It's not cricket to cut corners. So let's keep the ball rolling, right down to the finish line, and we'll have a field day.

These three sentences contain *nine* idioms from sports, and that's not a ballpark figure! They may not be a model of elegant prose—at *The New Yorker* they would say "Block that metaphor!"—but they show how terms from sports have become part of everyday speech.

All of the six hundred or so words and expressions in this book are associated with sports—most of them actually originated in one or another sport—but they have acquired far more extensive meaning. For example, a *southpaw* now simply means a left-handed person, whether or not he or she has ever picked up a baseball. Similarly, *hit and run* now just means the leaving the scene of a motor-vehicle accident, and most wearers of *boxer shorts* don't realize they are so called because prizefighters first wore them.

For the derivation and history of these words and phrases, I have relied on the standard sources used by most lexicographers, especially the *Oxford English Dictionary* (abbreviated *OED* in the text), and the work of modern linguists such as Eric Partridge, John Ciardi, and William Safire. I also have consulted the work of numerous sportswriters and sportscasters, from Grantland Rice and Red Barber to John Madden.

The entries are arranged in alphabetical order, letter by letter up to the comma in the case of inversion. Thus, if a comma is part of the term, as in *Winning isn't everything, it's the only thing*, the entry is alphabetized as though there were no comma; if it is not part of the term, as in *catch-up, to play*, alphabetization stops at the comma. Numerals are alphabetized as if they were written out (.400 is alphabetized as "four"). Alternative forms of an expression are indicated by a slash, as in *good loser/sport*. When there are several phrases around a central word, the term is alphabetized under that word; *in the money* and *out of the money* are found under *money, to finish in/out of the*. In cases where a reader is likely to look up an alternate word or would benefit from consulting a related expression, I have supplied a cross-reference, which is printed in SMALL CAPITALS (for example, *see also* FOUL OFF).

Because this system is imperfect, the reader who has trouble finding a term is advised to look in the index at the back of the book.

I am deeply indebted to the many sports-minded friends and acquaintances who originally inspired this project and then generously shared their expertise. Among them are my tennis partners of many years' standing, especially Lee Hatfield, Marita Hartshorn, Pat Lund, Pat McCoy, Mary Ellen Turner, and Jean Wanless. Special thanks are due to family friend and all-round athlete Jorge Rodriguez; hockey expert John J. McWeeney; soccer coach Robert T. Hartshorn; my husband and best singles opponent, Dean S. Ammer; our younger son and family baseball player, Dave Ammer; and most of all, our older son, John Ammer, hiker, runner, backpacker, canoeist, and tennis enthusiast, who patiently answered numerous questions and supplied some fascinating bits of information. This book is much better for their help. Its errors and shortcomings are solely my own.

SOUTHPAWS

&

SUNDAY PUNCHES

A A A A A

ace, to

To do extremely well; to get high marks. Although the noun *ace* was used in dice-playing as early as the 13th century, when it began to signify a throw of one, it was not used to describe an outstanding performer until World War I. The French called an airman who had shot down ten enemy planes *as*, a term quickly translated into English (*ace*) and applied to other kinds of expert. However, a century earlier an *ace* meant a winning point scored at racquets and badminton, and in the late 19th century it began to be used to describe an unreturnable stroke in these older racket sports and in tennis— particularly an unreturnable serve.

By the 1920's the expression had taken verbal form, *to ace* meaning to serve an ace. And in the mid-20th century it began to be used figuratively, to score high in any endeavor. Smart students might be said "to ace their final exam."

An ace still means an unreturnable serve in tennis, as well as a hole-in-one in golf. In baseball it generally means the best pitcher on a team. At least one writer believes this last sense was derived from Asa Brainard, who pitched for the Cincinnati Red Stockings. In 1869 that team won 56 out of a total of 57 games, using only Brainard as their pitcher, and, the writer claims, his name came to mean a good pitcher and was shortened to "Ace."

> *"The way his horses ran could be summed up in a word. Last."*
>
> —GROUCHO MARX, *Esquire*, 1972

across the board

Applying to all individuals, groups, or categories. The term comes from betting on horse races, where it signifies a combination bet on every winning possibility, that is, win (first place), place (second place), or show (third place). By the mid-20th century it was extended to other endeavors, particularly those involving money, such as an *across-the-board* price reduction (for all items being sold), wage increase (for all employees), or tax cut (for all tax brackets).

against the clock
In competition with the passage of time, so as to finish faster than anyone else, or by a certain time. This term comes from various athletic races in which the competitors are not lined up against one another but are timed individually, and the winner is the one with the best (fastest) time. This procedure is followed in contests ranging from running marathons, which follow a prescribed street course, to Olympic ski and skating races. In the mid-20th century the term began to be transferred to other endeavors, particularly those that involve meeting a deadline. For example, "The writers were working against the clock to come up with a new episode for *L.A. Law*" (*The Bulletin*, 1990).

ahead of/behind the count
In an advantageous/disadvantageous position. The term comes from baseball. A pitcher is said to be *ahead* of the count if he has thrown more strikes than balls. The reverse is true for a batter ahead of the count (more balls than strikes have been called). Conversely, a pitcher is *behind* the count when the umpire has called more balls than strikes, a situation similarly reversed for the batter. The term is used figuratively as well, as in "Marge has not only made up the assignments she missed, but she's way ahead of the count in her reading."

ain't over till it's over: *see* IT AIN'T OVER.

Alibi Ike
A person who constantly makes excuses for his or her shortcomings or failures. This term comes from the title and main character of a popular short story by Ring Lardner. Published in 1924, it tells of a ball player named Frank X. Farrell, who is constantly making excuses for himself and never accepts responsi-

bility for his mistakes. The story was made into a motion picture in 1932 with Joe E. Brown playing Alibi Ike, which helped establish the general use of the name as a term for a self-exonerating fast talker. However, it is heard less often today.

Ali shuffle

Exceptional nimbleness of foot. The term refers to boxer Cassius Clay, who adopted the Islamic name Muhammad Ali. Heavyweight champion from 1974 to 1978, Ali was famous for his fast talk (see I'M THE GREATEST) and his outstanding footwork. See also FANCY FOOTWORK.

all-out

Using all of one's strength or resources. Although the term was used as an adverb meaning "entirely" or "completely" as long ago as 1300, the present adjectival meaning of making an immense effort dates only from late 19th-century America and was originally used in athletics, particularly in races or other feats of physical exertion. "Irvine ... was willing ... to 'go all out,' as he put it, in an utmost attempt to reach the top," wrote E. F. Norton in his *Fight for Everest* (1925). Today we transfer such an effort to just about any enterprise. For example, one might make an all-out effort to produce a fuel-efficient automobile or a highly successful dinner party.

In cricket, incidentally, the term has a totally different meaning: A team that is "all out" is retired because each batsman has been dismissed.

> "So we won the first game. Some of the other players may have felt it was all over but the shouting, but I wasn't one of them. I thought the Red Sox woro a good team."
>
> —YOGI BERRA on the 1949 pennant race (*Yogi, It Ain't Over . . .* , 1989)

all over but the shouting

The result of a contest or an action appears to be certain. This term originated in 19th-century British sports; the *OED* cites its first use in Charles J. Apperley's *Life of a Sportsman* (1842). It soon was applied to other kinds of contest, particularly elections, and continues to be so used.

all-star
Consisting of the most outstanding performers. Although the word "star" was used for stage celebrities in Britain as long ago as 1779, it was first applied to outstanding athletes in the United States in the late 19th century and soon crossed the Atlantic. The first *all-star game*, featuring the outstanding baseball players of the year from the American and National Leagues, took place on July 6, 1933, in Chicago's Comiskey Park, and thereafter became an annual event. At first the all-star players were chosen by the fans; later the managers made the selection, and still later the players joined in the vote. Since 1970 this honor has been accorded by the fans, who vote by balloting. The term "all-star" soon was applied by advertisers to all varieties of entertainment, which often purport to present an *all-star cast*, and continues to be used in this way.

all the way, to go
To carry something to its conclusion. Although in Britain this term was used figuratively from the early 20th century on, in America it has definite associations with football, where it describes any play that scores a touchdown. Thus a player carrying the ball over the goal line is said to have gone all the way. By the mid-20th century the term also became a slang expression for performing sexual intercourse (as opposed to merely engaging in its preliminaries).

all-time
Unsurpassed; the greatest. This term originated in American sports in the early 20th century, and eventually described an actual listing of athletes. Babe Ruth was the first to make the *all-time list*. (When shortstop Johnny Logan was asked to name the greatest player ever, he came out with "I'll have to go with the immoral [sic] Babe Ruth.") However, the expres-

sion was soon transferred to other enterprises, such as an all-time high in automobile production, or used more loosely, as in an all-time favorite popular song.

also-ran

An unsuccessful competitor; a loser. The term comes from horse racing, where it is applied to a horse that either finishes out of the money (in fourth place or lower) or does not finish the race; it sometimes also is applied to a horse that is not expected to be among the top winners. The expression dates from the 1890's and comes from the racing results published in newspapers, which list for each race the horses that win, place, and show, followed by the rest under the heading "also ran." It was transferred first to athletes who did poorly in competition and later to losers of other contests (such as elections), as well as more broadly to persons who had little or no success in any field.

> "Amateur: one who plays games for the love of the thing. Unlike the professional, he receives no salary, and is contented with presents of clothes, clubs, rackets, cigarettes, cups, cheques, hotel expenses, fares, and so on."
>
> —J. B. MORTON, *Beachcomber* (1974)

amateur

One who cultivates a particular field of endeavor as a hobby or pastime. Today the word may also imply that such an individual is inexperienced or unskilled in the enterprise, that is, not good enough to be paid for it. Such a person is often called a *rank amateur*. Although the term was first used (about 1780) to describe individuals with a fondness for the arts (it comes from the Latin *amare*, "to love"), it was very soon thereafter used in sports, at first (about 1800) to distinguish gentlemen spectators from the participants in prizefights and then for athletes who participated for the fun of it—that is, gentlemen who did not have to earn their living.

It is this 19th-century meaning that long persisted in athletic contests, notably in tennis, where amateurs were players not paid to play and professionals received prize money and other forms of payment. Only amateurs were allowed to take part in grand-slam events (national championships) and Davis Cup competition, until 1968, when the distinction was officially eliminated. By then it had already been blurred, with players advertising or promoting various brands of equipment and receiving free training, travel expenses, and the like (see the quotation above). The distinction also persisted in the Olympic Games, which were confined to amateurs until recently. However, in these sports "amateur" did not usually have the disparaging connotation of inexperienced or inept, only unpaid vs. paid. In 1982 Jack Kelly, Jr., vice-president of the U.S. Olympic Committee, said, "Let's be honest. A proper definition of an amateur today is one who accepts cash, not checks" (*Sports Illustrated*, Feb. 8, 1982).

"The anchorwoman asks, 'If we use our imagination about West Virginia . . .' "

—BILL MCKIBBEN, *Reflections (Television),*
The New Yorker, March 9, 1992

anchorman/woman

American name for the host of a television news program (the British prefer "presenter"). Although an anchorman once denoted the sailor in charge of a ship's anchor, a usage now obsolete, in the early 20th century it was transferred to the end man in a tug-of-war, who secures the rope by tying it around his body. Somewhat later, in the 1930's, it also was used for the last person to race on a relay team. The TV anchorman, dating from the mid-1950's, was derived from these sports expressions and, like them, preserves the original literal meaning of *anchor* as a device that provides a firm hold for otherwise wandering or floating parts. By about 1970 the word *anchorwoman* came into use for women television hosts.

"She . . . did angle for me."
—WILLIAM SHAKESPEARE, *All's Well That Ends Well*, 5:3

angling

The act of trying to obtain something by sly or artful methods. This term, of course, is a figurative form of "fishing," as in "fishing for a compliment." (Although the word "fishing" refers to what has been a serious food-gathering occupation for thousands of years, "angling" is used more for the sport of fishing, and hence earns a place in this book.) Literally angling means the art or skill of catching fish with a rod, line, and hook, which may or may not be baited. The word itself comes from the Old English *angul*, for "hook." By the late 16th century the term was used figuratively, by Shakespeare and numerous other writers, as well as continuing to be used literally. Perhaps the earliest famous proponent of the sport was Izaak Walton, who wrote, "God never did make a more calm, quiet, innocent recreation than angling" (*The Compleat Angler*, 1653).

Annie Oakley

A free ticket to a performance of some kind. This American colloquialism was first used for free tickets to baseball games, and later was extended to free passes to stage performances or any other event. The name is that of a real-life 19th-century Western sharpshooter, Annie Oakley (1860–1926). For four decades she starred in Buffalo Bill's Wild West Show and showed off her skill by throwing a playing card in the air and shooting holes through all the pips. Because holes were punched in free tickets to prevent their resale, they resembled the target cards, whence the name.

après-ski

Describing a species of clothing, entertainment, and other pursuits appropriate after a day on the ski slopes. This term, French for "after ski(ing)," entered the English language in the early 1950's, promulgated mainly by advertisers of clothes, restaurants, nightclubs, and the like who were hawking their wares to the winter-resort crowd. A decade later it gave rise to such variants as *après-game* ("after the game") parties and *après-swim* ("after swimming") coverups (for bathing suits).

armchair quarterback

A kibitzer; a critic who allegedly knows better than either the participants or the experts. The word "armchair" has been used in Britain for sideline critics since the late 19th century; the *OED* cites a *Times-Register* entry of 1886 that has Mr. Chamberlain sneering at "arm-chair politicians." The addition of "quarterback," however, is purely American, referring to the leadership role of the football quarterback, and dates from the first half of the 20th century. See also MONDAY-MORNING QUARTERBACK.

"He usually played second cornet back of Oliver's lead, an alternately delicate assist and blasting support."
— BARRY ULANOV, *A History of Jazz in America* (1952)

assist, an

An act of assistance or support. This expression originally came from baseball, where it was first used in the 1870's in the specific meaning of helping a player either to score or to put out an opponent. As Arthur Guiterman put it, "He may not score, and yet he helps to Win/Who makes the Hit that brings the Runner in" (*A Poet's Proverbs*, 1924).

The term later began to be used with a similar meaning in numerous other sports as well—basketball (a pass that leads directly to the receiver's scoring), hockey (tipping or passing the puck to a teammate who scores a goal), lacrosse (passing to a teammate who scores without having to evade an opposing player), etc. Moreover, assists are credited to individual players and are noted in the record books.

A related baseball term is *unassisted*, which began to be used about 1880 for a player making a putout without help. While an unassisted double play is fairly spectacular, the much rarer unassisted triple play is still more dramatic. According to Paul Dickson, by 1990 it had occurred only eight times in major-league play.

Although today the use of the noun *assist* is largely North American, it occurred from the late 16th to early 17th centuries in Britain, where, however, it has largely died out.

at bay

Cornered; in great distress. This term comes from the sport of hunting, where it is used in two ways. *Standing at bay* describes the position of the hunted stag (or other animal) when it is cornered and faces the pursuing hounds. *To keep/be kept at bay* refers to the position of the pursuing hounds. The word itself comes from the Old French adjective *abai*, meaning "barking," an association that has been totally lost in the figurative term in current use. This usage, incidentally, has been around since the late 16th century. Edmund Spenser had it in his *A View of the Present State of Ireland* (1596): "All former purposes were blanked, the governor at a bay, etc."

> *"The not-so-secret secret of this year's Democratic Presidential campaign has been the reluctance of the party's A team to take the field."*
> —R. W. APPLE, JR., *New York Times*, Feb. 16, 1992

A team
The top tier of personnel available. The term comes from baseball, where it means the team made up of a club's best players. Also, during spring training, a ball club may divide the players into A and B teams for purposes of practicing against each other. The term "A team" was adopted by the military, specifically the U.S. Special Forces, where it signifies a handpicked unit of twelve men, and is also used more generally for the top individuals in any organization. Also see FIRST STRING.

athlete's foot
A contagious fungus infection affecting the skin of the feet. The popular name of this unpopular disorder, which dates from the 1920's, refers to the fact that the fungus thrives in the warm, humid conditions of locker rooms and gyms, where the infection is frequently spread. It is also called ringworm of the feet, or, more technically, tinea pedis. Although not considered a serious disorder, athlete's foot involves itching and scaling, and can be unpleasantly persistent despite treatment with antifungal ointments.

athletic supporter: *see* JOCKSTRAP

backpack, to

To maneuver outside a space shuttle with the aid of a portable
life-support system. This 1960's transfer of a hiking term was
coined for American astronauts. The sports usage of the expression, current in the United States since about 1910, is a
graphic description of an undertaking—carrying needed items
in a pack on one's back—that certainly predates the term by
many years. Possibly it originated as a translation of the German equivalent, *rucksack*, which was adopted into English
about the mid-19th century. That word continues to be used
on both sides of the Atlantic, although to American outdoor
aficionados it tends to denote a smaller, always frameless
knapsack as opposed to the larger, often frame-equipped back-
pack.

> *"Frank tried to take charge, back-pedaling quickly to
> the center of the room so he was next to his wife and
> facing Carver."*
>
> —JOHN LUTZ, *Hot* (1992)

back-pedal, to

To reverse course; to stop. Before bicycles were equipped
with hand brakes, pressing down and back on one pedal as it
rose was the standard way to stop. By about 1900, only a few
decades after the invention of this mode of transport, the
word *back-pedaling* was being used figuratively to mean reversing or retreating from one's previous stand, and it continued to be so used long after the early coaster brakes had been
replaced by hand brakes.

In addition to its figurative use, back-pedaling also has
literal meaning in several other sports. In boxing, it means retreating or backing away from one's opponent in the ring. In
football, it means running backward while facing an opponent

or a play in progress, a maneuver often executed by defensive backs who are guarding the opposing team's receivers.

back to back
Two consecutive events. The term originated about 1900 in baseball, where it means two consecutive hits of the same kind—for example, back-to-back homers (home runs hit by two consecutive batters). It is transferred to any similar situation, as in "The agent sold two of Mark's plays back to back."

bait, to
To tease, harass, or torment. The term comes from an ancient and cruel sport in which an animal such as a bear, bull, or badger was chained up, and dogs were set to attack it (the word *bait* comes from Old English and German words for "bite"). The earliest references to such baiting date from the 14th century. Bears actually were bred for baiting, and the spectators would bet on the outcome—that is, how many dogs would be killed before the bear was torn to pieces. Bull baiting was also common, the breed called *bulldog* being especially bred for it; it was slightly more humane, in that only one dog was set on the bull at one time (numerous dogs would be used against a bear). Badger baiting also was a popular sport. Nevertheless, Parliament outlawed bear baiting in 1835.

The term *baiting* was used figuratively by the mid-17th century and is still so used today, as, for example, "The boss has an unpleasant way of baiting his secretary."

ball boy
A flunky; one who performs menial tasks. The term originated around the turn of the 20th century. In America it meant, in both tennis and baseball, the individual, usually a boy or young man, who was charged with retrieving balls for the players (or, in baseball, for the umpire); in Britain it designated only the tennis-ball retriever. The term continues to be used, although from the mid-20th century on girls also per-

formed this function, giving rise to the term *ball girl*. By the mid-20th century the term was transferred to individuals performing similar tasks in other arenas, but this usage is not widespread. Also, today *bat boys* are more common than ball boys in baseball, although some teams have ball girls to retrieve the ball in foul territory.

> "*If people don't want to come to the ballpark, nobody's going to stop them.*"
> —YOGI BERRA, *It Ain't Over* (1989)

ballpark, in/out of the

A rough estimate; within a reasonable range. The transfer of ballpark, specifically meaning a baseball field, to general terminology dates from about 1960, and the word is used in two principal ways. *In* or *out of the ballpark* signifies that something is either approximately accurate (*in*) or is beyond a reasonable range (*out*). A closely related term, *ballpark figure*, means a roughly accurate approximation; it has been used since about 1970.

The transfer alludes to the fact that a ballpark is of necessity an enclosed space. Incidentally, the word *ballpark* has been exclusively used for a baseball field since the turn of the 20th century; it is never used for any other sports arena, at least not in North America.

ballpark figure: *see* BALLPARK, IN/OUT OF THE

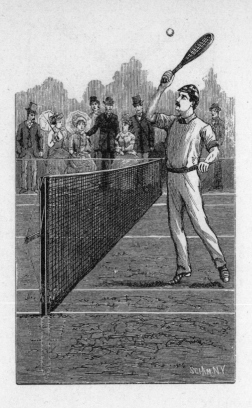

ball's in your court, the
It's your turn; it's up to you. This term comes from tennis, where it signifies that it is the opponent's turn to serve, return, or otherwise play the ball. A British equivalent is "the ball's at your feet," which comes from football (soccer), and has been in use much longer. Lord Auckland used it figuratively in a letter of about 1800: "We have the ball at our feet."

bare-knuckle
Rough, without niceties. The term comes from boxing, where until the late 19th century most bouts took place without any boxing gloves. The first generally recognized bare-knuckles champion in the United States was Paddy Ryan. In the first re-

corded fight, he won by knocking out Joe Goss of England in the eighty-seventh round; both he and Goss had placed bets on the outcome. Two years later, in 1882, Ryan was knocked out in the ninth round by John L. Sullivan, who was the last bare-knuckles boxing champion. His reign lasted a decade, until 1892.

Although opinion is divided, some authorities believe that bare-knuckle bouts were actually less brutal and injurious than boxing with gloves. According to Harry Carpenter, "The glove is there to guard the hand from damage, not add to its power. Therein lies the demarcation line between boxing today and boxing yesterday" (*Boxing: An Illustrated History*, 1982). Nevertheless, the figurative use of bare knuckles has survived, as in "Enter [Vice-President Dan] Quayle, the feisty finger-pointing, scrappy conservative in search of a bare-knuckles brawl" (*Boston Globe*, June 11, 1992).

Under the London Prize Ring Rules, whenever a contender was down, whether or not he had been hit or had simply fallen down, he was allowed thirty seconds before being called out. In effect, a fighter could rise and immediately fall down again, getting thirty more seconds of rest, repeating the process until he felt able to resume fighting. The Marquis of Queensberry Rules, which came into general use in 1892, required the use of gloves, as well as three-minute rounds and a limit of ten seconds after being knocked down.

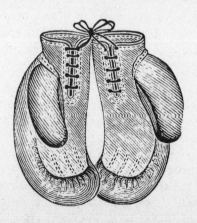

"Baseball caps are high style these days. . . .such an above-the-waist mega-fashion spanning both sexes, all incomes, and every age."
—GAIL BANKS, *Boston Globe Magazine* (May 3, 1992)

baseball cap

A cap with a deep visor that usually bears some name, slogan, or other emblem. A basic part of the baseball uniform since the 19th century, it had become a generic name for that kind of cap by the mid-20th century. In sports the cap displays the name or emblem of a particular team. In general use, however, it has become a vehicle for advertising just about any product, saying, or organization, and also is available without any inscription. The version with a tractor company logo also became known as a *gimme cap*, because farmers often told a tractor salesman, "Gimme one of those."

baseball diplomacy

American efforts to ease international tensions. This term was coined in 1971 by East European journalists, expressing their more or less shocked reaction to President Richard Nixon's announced plans to visit the Republic of China, with which the United States had had virtually no formal relations since the Communists took it over after World War II. It was translated into English (from its first appearance in Polish and Hungarian newspapers) but never came into wide use in America. The reference to baseball here is a synonym for "American" rather than to any specific features of the game. See also under PING-PONG.

bat around, to

To consider various alternatives in a haphazard way. The term comes from baseball practice, or more likely, from a sandlot or pickup baseball game, and is used chiefly in North America. In the late 19th century it also had another meaning, to move or wander about in idle fashion. William Dean Howells used it in this way in a 1907 letter to Mark Twain: "She was in England ... batting round with two other girls and having a great time." This usage is still current but not common.

*"Hitting is the hardest thing in baseball. . . . Ted Williams
said that it was the hardest thing in sports, because if
you did it three times out of ten you were very good."*

—YOGI BERRA

batting average

One's record of success or failure. The term comes from baseball, whose devotees are particularly addicted to record-
keeping. To calculate the batting average, divide the number
of base hits by the number of official times at bat and carry
the result to three decimal places. ("Official times" are only
those when a batter hits the ball or strikes out; walks and sac-
rifices do not count.) Thus 1.000 would be a perfect batting
record, and it has never been attained. Nevertheless, the figurative term, *batting 1.000* (pronounced "one thousand" despite the decimal point), is used to describe someone who has
a perfect record or has achieved a flawless performance.

The literal term has been in use since the 1860's. The
highest batting average ever achieved in a single season was
.438 by Hugh Duffy of the Boston Beaneaters in 1894. At this
writing the last average over .400 was .406 by Ted Williams of
the Boston Red Sox in 1941, and as Berra points out above,
Williams himself considered anything over .300 extremely
good.

In cricket the batting average is calculated by dividing
the number of runs a batsman has scored by the number of
completed innings he has had; thus 2,400 runs in 40 innings
would mean a batting average of 60.

batting order

A fixed sequence of events. This term, too, comes from baseball, where the order in which the players go to bat is determined at the beginning of a game and may not be changed. In
cases of substitution, the substitute goes to bat in the order of
the player he replaces.

The figurative use of batting order is strictly American.
Britons would consider it a cricket term with a necessarily
different meaning, since in cricket the order of batsmen is less

rigidly fixed. They come to bat only once during an innings (which often constitutes an entire match), and the order of those who have not yet batted can be changed in the course of the innings.

> *"Though Luther, Zwinglius, Calvin, holy chiefs,*
> *Have made a battel Royal of beliefs."*
>
> —JOHN DRYDEN, *The Hind and the Panther* (1687)

battle royal

A general fight; a heated argument. The term comes from cockfighting, where it is used for a fight involving several combatant cocks (not just two). In such a fight the single surviving cock is the victor. The term has been used figuratively since the mid-17th century and continues to be current even in places where cockfighting is now a rarity or completely unknown.

bat two for three, three for four, etc., to

To be relatively successful but not perfect. The expression, from baseball, indicates a player's success relative to the number of times at bat; two for three means he has two hits in three times at bat, etc. See also BATTING AVERAGE.

> *"I merely said that more than 34,000 people in the*
> *stands and the Red Sox players seemed to think it was*
> *a beanball."*
>
> —Broadcaster JIMMY BRITT, on Yankee
> pitcher Joe Page's throw, May 2, 1948

bean, to

To hit someone on the head, especially with a thrown object. This slang locution comes from baseball, where a *beanball* is a ball intentionally pitched directly at or very close to the batter's head in order to intimidate him. The verb form was already around in 1910, when an article in *American Magazine* defined it: "He is in extreme danger of being 'beaned,' which, in baseball, means hit in the head." The figurative noun "beanball" similarly means a direct shot, verbal or physical, that is intended to do damage, as in "The Democratic leadership pitched a beanball to the President's tax package."

"He bet about the bush, whyles others caught the birds."

—GEORGE GASCOYNE, *Works* (1572)

beat around the bush, to
To approach in a cautious or circuitous way; to shilly-shally. This expression for overcautiousness dates from the early 16th century. John Ciardi suggested that it probably comes from a hound pursuing game but veering around bushes and other obstacles and thereby letting the quarry get away. Or the saying may refer to beaters who fear that a dangerous animal might be concealed in bushes and therefore avoid them. Indeed, there are numerous sayings concerning the delays caused by too much beating and not enough bird-catching, dating from as early as 1300. "One man beats the bushes while another gets the bird" appears in numerous writings and languages, including several proverb collections. The British usually substitute *about* for *around*, as Robert Whytynton did in *Vulgaria* (1520): "A longe betynge aboute the busshe and losse of time." See also BEAT THE BUSHES FOR.

"Where if you beat a bush, 'tis odds you start a thief."
—MICHAEL DRAYTON, *Plyolbion* (1612)

beat the bushes for, to
To search for; to look hard for something. This term, like its close relative, BEAT AROUND THE BUSH, comes from the practice of having beaters flush game out for a hunting party. Here, however, the literal meaning of an exhaustive search has been transferred more directly to figurative use. For example, a candidate may be said to beat the bushes for campaign funds.

*"The tracking station at Plumeur Bodou is the place
that so exultantly beat Britain to the punch in getting
the first pictures from America via satellite."*
                                        —*The Listener,* 1965

beat to the punch, to

To achieve something faster or sooner than someone else.
This 20th-century term originated in America, where "to
beat" has meant "to surpass" since the late 18th century. It
comes from boxing, where it literally means to score with a
punch faster or earlier than one's opponent can land one. H. C.
Witwer used it in *Fighting Blood* (1923): "I beat Hanley to
the punch ... and he went down on his haunches" (cited by
the *OED*).

"Because it's there"

Explanation for attempting a difficult or seemingly pointless
feat; also, a more general evasive reply. It is a direct quotation of a statement attributed to British mountaineer George
Leigh Mallory (1886–1924), made during an American lecture
tour in 1923. When asked why he was attempting to climb
Mount Everest, this was his reply, as reported in John Hunt's
account, *The Ascent of Everest* (1954). Mallory did not succeed; in fact, he vanished during the climb and his body was
never recovered. However, his statement was not forgotten.
It was repeated by the first man to succeed in climbing the
mountain, Sir Edmund Hillary, in 1953. When announcing his
plans, he was asked the same question and gave the same answer. Later the phrase was transferred to other enterprises,
most often in humorous or ironic fashion, and it came to be
used as either a rationalization for foolish behavior or an
ironic answer to a silly question.

beer and skittles, not all

Not all fun and games; a serious business. This term, originally British and still used more widely there than in America, characterizes the easy life as meaning plenty to drink and
pleasurable games. Skittles is a target game that involves

propelling a ball or other projectile against wooden pins. Extremely popular throughout Europe during the Middle Ages, skittles was often played in taverns, whence the association with beer. It also frequently involved betting, and for this reason it was forbidden in the City of London in 1800.

Dickens used the phrase "porter and skittles" in his *Pickwick Papers* (1837), and two decades later Thomas Hughes had the modern negative version in *Tom Brown's School Days* (1857), "Life isn't all beer and skittles." By this time *skittles* had acquired the colloquial meaning of "nonsense" or "rubbish," and hence the figurative sense of beer and skittles, that is, something pleasurable but trivial.

"*Right now we're behind the eight ball.*"
—ERLE STANLEY GARDNER, *The D.A. Goes to Trial* (1940)

behind the eightball
In a bad situation; bad luck. This term originated in the United States in the first half of the 20th century and comes from a form of pool in which all the balls must be pocketed in a certain order. The only exception is the No. 8 ball, or eightball, which is black. If another player touches the eightball, he or she is penalized. Therefore, if the eightball is in front of the ball one is supposed to pocket next, one is in a difficult spot—that is, right behind the eightball.

"*He can't see a belt without hitting below it.*"
—MARGOT ASQUITH, about David Lloyd George

below the belt
Unfair behavior. The expression comes from boxing and refers to the Marquis of Queensberry Rules, which prohibit striking an opponent there. From 1743 on boxing, or prizefighting as it was then usually called, was governed by the London Prize Ring Rules. These regulations provided for fighting with bare fists (see BARE-KNUCKLE) and allowed wrestling, biting, scratching, and gouging. Fights ended in a knockout, unless the authorities intervened, and there were

no time limits. A round ended whenever one contender fell to the ground.

John Sholto Douglas, Marquis of Queensberry (1844–1900), objected to the brutality of this sport and, assisted by Arthur Chambers, formulated a new set of rules in 1865. They required fighters to wear leather gloves and to fight in a 24-foot ring for three-minute rounds, with one-minute rest periods between rounds. The only offensive maneuvers allowed were striking with the closed fist at the opponent's upper body or head. Although not fully accepted at first, the Queensberry Rules gradually gained ground, and by about 1885 they were being adopted on both sides of the Atlantic. By then, also, *hitting below the belt* began to be used figuratively for any kind of unfair action or statement.

> *"All players and substitutes of the side at bat must be seated on their team's bench."*
> —*Spalding's Baseball Guide* (1916)

bench, on the

A figurative place for a nonparticipant; on the sidelines; also, held in reserve. This term comes from baseball, football, and other sports in which players may literally sit on a bench during a game, waiting to be called in to play. Originally those on the bench were simply awaiting their turn. As teams grew to include more players for use in specific situations, there were more and more temporarily unneeded team members owing to the particular circumstances of a game or the fact that they were playing poorly. This practice gave rise to such related terms as *benchwarmer*, one who remains on the bench for a long time (a whole game, several games, an entire season); such a player is also said to RIDE THE BENCH. In figurative usage, the most common terms are *on the bench* and the verb *to bench* (or *to be benched*), all meaning to be set aside as a nonparticipant, either temporarily or permanently.

bench jockey

A person who harasses active participants from the sidelines. The term comes from baseball, where it is used for a player who loudly criticizes the opposing team and/or the umpires from the bench or dugout.

> *"Though nobody in the modern world holds a monopoly on sports frenzy, the Big Game happens only in America."*
>
> —E. H. CADY, *The Big Game: College Sports and American Life* (1978)

big game

A major goal or target, especially one that involves risk. The term comes from hunting, where big game refers to the large wild animals hunted for sport, such as lions, tigers, antelope, or bear. It has been used figuratively since the first half of the 20th century, as in "He's out for big game now; he has his eye on the boss's own account."

Together with the article "the," the term also acquired another meaning, that is, the most important athletic competition (football game, basketball game, etc.) of a college season, often the one against a traditional rival (see the quotation above).

bigger they come (the harder they fall), the

Those in high positions have more to lose when they fail. This term is believed to come from boxing and has been attributed to several contenders. Among them is British-born boxer Bob Fitzsimmons (1862–1917), who defeated world heavyweight champion James J. Corbett in 1897 but lost to James J. Jeffries two years later. It also has been attributed to heavyweight champion John L. Sullivan (1877–1918) but is probably proverbial.

> *"... and, funniest of all, sold this package to the people with such success that the Democrats' big hitters all decided they would rather 'spend more time with the family' in 1992 than challenge him."*
>
> —JAMES RESTON on George Bush, *New York Times*, Sept. 20, 1991

big hitter

A very powerful and/or influential person. The expression comes from baseball, where, as New York Giants manager Leo Durocher once said, "There are only five things you can do in baseball—run, throw, catch, hit, and hit with power" (*Time*, July 16, 1973). Or, as home-run king Babe Ruth put it, "I swing big, with everything I've got. I hit big or I miss big. I like to live as big as I can" (quoted in William and Leonard Safire's *Words of Wisdom*). See also HEAVY HITTER.

> "A ball player's got to be kept hungry to become a big leaguer. That's why no boy from a rich family ever made the big leagues."
> —Attributed to New York Yankees outfielder JOE DIMAGGIO

big league

Among the foremost; the highest level of any undertaking. The term comes from baseball, where it is a synonym for MA-JOR LEAGUE. See also MINOR LEAGUE. The figurative use of the expression dates from the first half of the 20th century. It is used in various forms—*the big league*, for the big time; *big-league*, describing an important person or enterprise; and *big-leaguer*, one employed by a very important or powerful organization.

bird-dog, to

To follow closely or watch carefully. The term comes from the sport of hunting, and refers to a dog especially trained to flush out and retrieve game birds. Sometimes called *gun dogs*, such animals have been known as bird dogs, principally in North America, since the late 19th century. The term had been transferred to more general usage by 1950.

As a noun the term is used in at least two other sports. In golf a *bird dog* denotes a particularly good caddie; in baseball a *bird dog* is a scout sent out to observe and recruit new talent for a team (or, alternatively, to report on the players and strategies of opposing teams).

black belt

An expert of the top rank. The term comes from judo and other Asian arts of self-defense, where different grades of achievement are rewarded with the privilege of wearing a waistband or sash of a particular color, with a black belt signifying the highest level of skill. The term began to denote other kinds of expertise in the second half of the 20th century.

blanket finish

A very close finish; virtually a tie. The term comes from horse racing and alludes to competitors so close at the finish line that a single blanket could cover them. See also BY A NOSE; CLOSE FINISH.

> *"Some think that, by going to work at eight, they may adjourn to the bleachers or the teeing-ground at half-past three."*
>
> —*New York Evening Post,* May 13, 1909

bleachers

Inexpensive seats for a performance. The term was first used in the late 19th century for the cheapest seats in a baseball park. They consisted of simple wooden benches made from what were called *bleaching boards*, which was shortened to bleachers. One theory holds that the "bleaching" referred to the lightening of the wood as it was exposed to sun and rain; another contends that "bleacher" is a jocular reference to the seats' occupants, who themselves were bleached by the elements. Although the word is still used mainly for this section of athletic stadiums, it also has been applied to the viewing stands used for parades as well as the cheap seats in night-clubs and theaters.

blind-side, to

To launch a sneak attack; to take advantage of a person's weakness. The term comes from football and other contact sports, where it means to tackle or block a player from the blind side—that is, away from where he or she is looking. It

began to be used figuratively from the 1970's on. For example, "[He] asked whether those Republicans who stand with
the President were going to be 'blindsided' by any more
bombs" (*Newsweek*, Dec. 3, 1973; cited by *OED*).

> *"In the early stages of developing a [business] format,
> the concept is paramount. But when there are imita-
> tors out there, it becomes a boring game of blocking
> and tackling."*
>
> —Retail analyst DAVID BOLOTSKY, quoted
> in *Boston Globe*, June 9, 1992

block, to

To bring to a halt; to obstruct. Although this verb has been
used since the late 13th century in the meaning of placing an
obstacle in the way of something or someone—it comes from
various medieval words for stump or log—its use in American
football during the 20th century was a major impetus to its
widespread transference. For example, *The New Yorker* magazine has long used the headline "Block That Metaphor!" for
particularly illogical mixed figures of speech sent in by read-
ers. In football, blocking, which consists of linemen overpowering opposing linemen with a body or shoulder charge, is
perfectly legal, provided the blocker does not use his hands.
"To me, the most important thing about any [football] play
was the blocking," wrote John Madden. "If you don't block
properly, the play can't possibly work (*Hey, Wait a Minute*,
1984).

In cricket, blocking is also legal; here it denotes stopping
a ball with the bat in order to protect the wicket (without trying to hit the ball so as to score a run). In basketball, it can
denote either a legal blocking of an offensive shot or an illegal
movement in the opponent's path; with the latter, the player
doing so is charged with a personal foul. In baseball, it denotes a fielder preventing a runner from touching a base in an
obstructive way, and also is illegal.

blow-by-blow

A detailed description. This term, originating in America in the early 1930's, comes from radio broadcasts giving a detailed account of the punches struck in a prizefight ("A right to the body, a left to the chin, etc."). The journal *American Speech* defined the term in 1933. In the next few decades it was transferred to a detailed account of just about any event, as, for example, a blow-by-blow description of a job interview, a dinner party, or a movie plot. See also PLAY-BY-PLAY.

boat people

Refugees who flee their homeland by putting to sea in boats, which often are unable to land because no nation wants to take them in. This term of the 1980's is an ironic transfer of sporting boat people—that is, the yachting set, who unlike the refugees, represent a wealthy and often socially prominent social group. This term came into use about the late 1960's, for refugees from Southeast Asian countries, and was applied to Haitian refugees in the early 1990's. Still earlier, in the late 19th century, the expression designated Chinese people who permanently lived in houseboats or junks.

bob and weave, to

To move erratically or evasively in constantly changing directions. The term comes from boxing, where a fighter evades his opponent by moving the head and upper body back and forth, and up and down, quickly and repeatedly. "Keep weaving and bobbing at a comfortable pace," instructs J. O'Brien's *Boxing* (1928). By the second half of the 20th century the term had been transferred to any kind of erratic movement, as in "Production bobs and weaves from week to week" (*Business Week*, Aug. 4, 1975; cited by *OED*). In baseball the term "bob and weave" is occasionally used for a knuckleball, on account of its erratic path.

body blow

An extremely damaging action. The term comes from boxing, where it simply means a punch to the opponent's body somewhere between breastbone and navel. The boxing term dates from the 18th century. It began to be used figuratively about 1900, as in, for example, "The strike dealt a body blow to the railroad owners."

body English

Movements of the body that convey particular feelings or intentions. The term dates from the turn of the 20th century and comes from such sports as bowling and hockey, where the player makes an instinctive attempt to influence the movement of a ball or puck by contorting the body in one direction or another. The word *English* alone has long been used in billiards and other sports to denote spin imparted to a ball, and it is this sense that gave rise to "body English."

> *"Get out of here before you make any more boners."*
> —VIRGINIA PERRDUE, *The Case of the Grieving Monkey* (1941)

boner

A stupid mistake. This term comes from baseball, along with *bonehead*, a person who makes a bad error. The latter actually was used earlier in the 19th century to describe stubbornness as well as stupidity; A. J. Dickson had it in *Across the Plains* (1864), "Some boneheaded mule displayed characteristic traits." However, it was revived in early 20th-century baseball in a newspaper item describing a famous play. Fred Merkle, New York Giants first baseman, did not touch second base in the deciding game of the championship series at New York's Polo Grounds on Sept. 23, 1908. His mistake cost his team the game and resulted in a riot, and Charles Dryden, writing about the play, described Merkle as a "bonehead." From this came the use of "boner" for a stupid mistake, later extended to any dumb action or remark, whose perpetrator still is described as a bonehead.

bookie

Also, *bookmaker.* A person who is in the business of accepting
and paying off the bets of others. In early English horse racing, when friend raced friend, it became customary for each of
them to make a side bet, which was paid off when the race
was won. As the sport grew and strangers raced one another,
eager to bet but not trusting each other, the money was
posted with a reputable person, who was called the "stakes
holder." As racing became more popular and wagers increased, the stakes holders protested against continuing to do
this work without pay, and to placate them they were offered
a percentage, normally 5 percent, of the total stake. In time
this method, too, was insufficient to meet demand. Enough
bets were made so that a record had to be kept. This record
began to be called a *book* in Britain about 1800, and soon
thereafter *making book,* or *bookmaking,* began to be used for
receiving bets. In the mid-19th century the person who did so
began to be called a *bookmaker,* which was shortened to
bookie. This kind of formal betting, against agreed-on odds,
was preponderantly on horse races, and indeed in Britain the
only legally recognized method of handling such bets is by a
licensed *turf accountant.* However, informal betting on the
outcome of other sports events—boxing bouts, cricket
matches, boat races, football games—became increasingly
popular on both sides of the Atlantic. By the mid-20th century
one could place bets with a bookie on the outcome of many
other kinds of contest, such as elections (in deference to this
expansion the British now also call a bookie a *commission
agent*).

For horse races and prizefights, a bookie sets individual
odds for each competitor and keeps a record (book) of the bets
as they are made. The book is balanced so that no matter who
wins, the bookie will profit because the amount paid out on
winning bets is covered by that taken in on losing ones. The
percentage of the bookie's profit is, of course, calculated in
setting the odds and is generally a good deal higher than 5
percent. The bookie pays off a bet at the odds as they were at
the time the bet was placed, regardless of how they might

later change. For games like football and basketball, the bookie usually establishes a point spread instead of setting separate odds for each team. The odds will remain fixed, but the point spread will vary as necessary to balance winning bets against losing ones and ensure a profit for the bookie. From this comes the related expression, to *make book on* something, meaning to stand ready to quote odds on a bet on any competitor, or, by extension, to bet confidently or be able to rest assured (as bookies generally are of their profit).

"You certainly did bowl her over uncommon well."
　　　　　　　—ANTHONY TROLLOPE, *The Claverings* (1867)

bowled over, to be

To be figuratively overwhelmed or greatly surprised. This term began to be used in Britain in the mid-19th century and came from cricket, where "bowling an over" has a special meaning. There are two bowlers (counterparts of baseball's pitcher) and each bowls to the opposing batsman six times, which constitutes an *over*. If the batsman does not make a single run during an over, the bowler is said to have *bowled a maiden over*. A bowler also may succeed in bowling a batsman *out*, that is, get him out by bowling the bails off the wicket. From these expressions came the figurative usage, first of *bowling a person out*, meaning to get rid of someone, and then *bowling someone over*.

"Three things are thrown away in a bowling-green, namely, time, money, and oaths."
　　　　　　　—WALTER SCOTT, *The Fortunes of Nigel* (1822)

Bowling Green

The name of a town in Kentucky, a town and a university in Ohio, a small park at the southern end of New York's Borough of Manhattan, and other places as well. All these come from the 17th-century name for the smooth, level lawn used for the game of bowls (also called *lawn bowling* or *bowling on the green*), and the Manhattan park originally was a field so used.

Extremely popular in Tudor times, when it was also called *crown-green bowls*, the game involves rolling one's ball to a point as close as possible to a white ball at the end of the green. Although it is no longer as popular as in earlier times, it is still played in some parts of the world.

boxer shorts

Also, *boxers*. Loose-fitting undershorts of cotton or a similar lightweight material with an elastic waistband. The name comes from their resemblance to the shorts worn by prize-fighters. This type of men's underwear became popular after World War I. Before 1900 men wore woolen underwear. The earliest boxer shorts were made of silk or Egyptian cotton and had buttons and a tab rather than an elastic waist. Actually, the first references to them by this name in print date from the early 1940's. In the second half of the 20th century they were largely displaced by closer-fitting cotton knit underwear, but in the mid-1980's they began to become popular again. One company, the Joe Boxer Corporation, announced in 1992 that 18 percent of American men today wear boxers, compared to 11 percent in 1986. American women were taking to them as well, but generally for use as sportswear (shorts). Fashion designer Calvin Klein said that by 1988, 20 to 25 percent of his boxers were being purchased by women. Rather than being made of plain white cloth, today's boxers often sport printed patterns and bright colors; one store's best-selling kind had a palm-tree print.

> "*A baseball box score is a democratic thing. It doesn't tell how big you are ... what color you are ... just what kind of baseball player you were on that particular day.*"
>
> —JACKIE ROBINSON quoting Branch Rickey,
> *I Never Had It Made* (1972)

box score

A detailed record of an event; a summary of the results. The term is a figurative version of the baseball box score, a statis-

tical summary in table form that has been used since the early
20th century to record the essential details of a game. It includes the names and position of each team's players, the batting order, and their performance during the game (number of
times at bat, runs, hits, errors, runs batted in). Similar sum-
maries are used in other sports, especially basketball. The expression was being used figuratively by the 1930's and is
particularly popular with elected officials referring to their
own record. Among those who so used it were Presidents
Franklin D. Roosevelt, Harry S. Truman, and more recently,
George Bush.

break cover, to
To emerge suddenly from concealment. The term comes from
hunting, where since the late 16th century it has been used to
describe a fox, rabbit, or other game animal starting forth
from its hiding place in the underbrush. By the turn of the
20th century the term was being transferred to other break-
outs from hiding, as in "Dr. Watson decided to discard his disguise, since he had already broken cover by responding when
addressed by his real name."

breaks, the (lucky)
Good fortune. The term apparently was first used in baseball
in the early 20th century, when it was used to describe a
game that turned out well, often because of a mistake by the
opponents. It soon was extended to other events and circumstances, and is still used informally in this way. However, it
also can refer simply to a less fortunate fate, as in "That flat
tire made me miss my plane—well, that's the breaks." See
also LUCKY BREAK.

breeze (through), to
To win easily. This term also was first used in baseball. "Won
it *in a breeze*" appeared in a 1910 issue of a baseball magazine,
and *it was a breeze* is also often heard. All these locutions,
which presumably allude to the quick, easy passage of a
breeze of air, were transferred to other enterprises, as in

"Mary claims to have breezed through her final exam; at least, she told her friends it was a breeze."

Bronx cheer
A loud, derisive sound made with the tongue and lips. Although this form of expressing contempt is surely much older, the name is believed to come from its use in New York's Yankee Stadium, located in the Borough of the Bronx and long the home of the New York Yankees baseball team. The term has been around since the early 1920's and was quickly applied to similar audience reaction in theaters, nightclubs, etc. The same noise has also been called a *raspberry* or *razzberry* since the late 19th century, but this term designated jeers directed at any kind of performer. See also RAZZ.

buck fever
Nervous excitement concerning any new experience. This Americanism of the early 19th century was first used for a novice hunter who becomes so unnerved at the sight of large game—such as his first buck, or stag—that he either misses his shot or forgets to shoot. It was soon transferred to a display of nerves by any beginner.

> "*Ms. Robertson writes that Seymour Topping, a former managing editor of the paper, frequently said that if Ms. Wade were not a woman, 'she'd be in the bullpen.'* "
> —SUSAN JACOBY, *New York Times,* March 19, 1992

bullpen
A place occupied by key personnel. The term comes from the fenced-off place where relief pitchers limber up during a baseball game. As for the importance of pitchers, Yogi Berra put it very succinctly in 1973: "If you ain't got a bullpen, you ain't got nothin'." Originally, of course, the term designated an animal enclosure, and it was transferred to other kinds of enclosure—prison cells, guardhouses, bunkhouses—during the

course of the 19th century, but virtually none of these applications remains current.

The exact origin of the usage in baseball is disputed. In the 1870's the term was used in some ballparks for a low-cost area for spectators, into which they were "herded like bulls in a pen." A later and both popular and plausible theory holds that it comes from the large advertising billboards for Bull Durham Tobacco (and other products) that loomed over ballpark fences. The Bull Durham Tobacco ads featured a huge, brightly colored bull, and because relief pitchers often warmed up in the shade cast by the large billboard, their area came to be called the bullpen. To further its cause the company indulged in a master stroke of public relations: It offered a prize to any player who batted a ball into one such bull—$50 and two bags of Bull Durham Tobacco.

bull's-eye, to score a
To make a direct hit—verbal, physical, or other; to make an exceptionally skillful stroke. The term comes from target practice, where the black center of a target marked with concentric circles has been called a bull's-eye since about 1800. While one might argue that target practice was mainly a military pursuit, targets are also used in the sports of archery and riflery. The term was being used figuratively by the mid-19th century. An 1857 collection of George Eliot's letters has: "The public is a very curious animal and . . . how difficult it is to tell what will hit a bull's eye" (cited by *OED*).

> "The minor leagues were out in the bushes. Calling someone bush is not a good thing to do unless you know him well or are bigger."
> —YOGI BERRA, *It Ain't Over* (1989)

bush league
Also, *bush*. Small-time, amateurish, not up to the highest standards. In baseball a bush league is a small minor league of low or mediocre quality, "bush" here taking on the meaning of "countrified" and "unimportant." The term, in use since the early 1900's, was transferred to other enterprises soon there-

after, as in references to "a bush theatrical production," or "a bush-league restaurant."

butterfingers
An individual who is apt to drop things; a clumsy person. The term, alluding to fingers made slippery with butter, was used of clumsy cricket players in Britain in the early 19th century—Dickens had it in *Pickwick Papers* (1837)—and was very quickly transferred to any clumsy individual (Thackeray so described an executioner handling the heads of those he had beheaded in 1840). In America it was similarly used for baseball players unable to catch well and then extended to any physically inept individual.

by a nose
Just barely. The term comes from horse racing and alludes to a horse that wins by inches, that is, the length of its nose. It began to be used about 1900 and soon was transferred to other kinds of close finish. See also BLANKET FINISH.

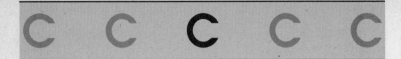

caddie
A person who runs errands or does odd jobs. The term comes from golf, where it signifies a person hired to carry the golfer's clubs and chase down lost balls. Although caddies today are rarer than they used to be, having been largely replaced by the CADDIE CART (itself sometimes shortened to "caddie") and GOLF CART, they are not entirely obsolete.

caddie cart
A rigid, two-wheeled vehicle for carrying heavy objects, such as luggage. The term refers to an identical device originally made for golfers to carry their clubs around the course. In contrast to the electric GOLF CART, it is powered by human muscle and consequently gives golfers more exercise than they would get by riding in a cart. First invented in the mid-20th century, the caddie cart soon was extended to other uses, such as carrying bags or moving any heavy object. Its name is therefore also shortened to *caddie* or given a more specific description, as in *luggage caddie*.

call 'em as I/you see 'em, I/you
This is my (your) view of the situation, no matter what anyone else thinks. The saying, widespread in many American sports, is the classic defense put up by umpires, referees, and linespersons in baseball, basketball, tennis, and just about any sport in which someone officiates and his or her decisions are occasionally disputed. It has been transferred to numerous other matters of judgment, not only as a defense but as an instruction to use one's own judgment.

call the game, to
Also, *called game*. To declare the end of some enterprise. The term comes from baseball and other sports, where an umpire rules that a game must end owing to weather conditions,

darkness, or some similar circumstance. An unusual situation arose in 1938, when a dust storm struck in Florence, South Carolina, during an exhibition game between the Boston Red Sox and Cincinnati Reds. In a freak occurrence, it caused every fly ball hit into the strong wind to be blown so far that it was lost. By the eighth inning, with the score tied at 18–18, the umpire called the game because they had run out of balls.

A few years ago Princeton economics professor Alan S. Blinder told his students that "the game was called" with reference to a department picnic that had been rained out.

call the shots, to
To exercise control over events; to make crucial decisions. This Americanism comes from certain forms of pool or billiards, such as straight pool, in which the player is required to specify both the ball he or she intends to pocket and the particular pocket. In the mid-20th century the expression began to be transferred to other enterprises, as in "As to where

we'll go for our vacation, it's Mom who is calling the shots this year."

call the signals, to
To decide the course of action. The term comes from football, where the quarterback or defensive captain uses a coded series of words and numbers to call for a specific play, formation, and the like. Originally it was the quarterback who both selected the plays and called them. In professional football today, it is usually the coaches who make the decision, but the quarterback still calls the plays via agreed-on signals. Frequently the "signals" refer just to the snap count. Sometimes, after seeing the defensive alignment, the quarterback will want to change the play that was called in the huddle. In this case the signals called will indicate the new situation (calling an "audible").

The actual signals consist of a series of numbers and one-syllable words. For example, John Madden described a Raiders play "Eighteen bob odd O." According to the team playbook, *eighteen* meant the halfback would carry the ball on a sweep around the right end; *bob* told the fullback to block the linebacker outside the Raiders right end; *odd* told the offensive linemen how to block (tight end on defensive end, right tackle on defensive tackle, right guard to lead interference for the halfback); and *O* told the left (offside) guard to pull and follow the right guard. After calling the play, the quarterback calls the snap count, "on one," "on two," "on three," or occasionally "on four." That means when he is at the line of scrimmage and yells "Hut, hut, hut . . ." the center will snap the ball on the first, second, etc. "hut," depending on which number was called.

"Calling the signals" was transferred to more generalized use about the mid-20th century, as in "I'm not sure which attorney will take the depositions; the senior partner is calling the signals."

can't hit the broad side of a barn
Describing an individual who has very poor aim or is hope-lessly incompetent. This hyperbole comes from baseball, where it was (and still is) applied to an unsuccessful or incom-petent pitcher. It may have originated there or come from other pursuits, such as poor target shooting. A similar de-scription of incompetence, *can't punch his way out of a paper bag*, comes from boxing. It, too, is a gross exaggeration.

can't lay a glove on (someone)
Describing someone who can do no harm whatever. The term comes from prizefighting, where it describes the boxer who cannot connect or land a punch on his opponent. The converse, to *lay a glove on* someone, means to land a punch. Both have been used figuratively, as in "Even if I flunk this course the dean can't lay a glove on me."

> *"He's blest who bears away the ball."*
> —SADI (GULISTAN), C. 1258

carry the ball, to
To take charge, to advance a cause. The term comes from football and rugby, where the ball-carrier executes a running play (see also RUN WITH THE BALL) that gives his team yard-age or even a touchdown. Carrying the ball is illegal in some games, such as basketball, but carrying it *away* meant win-ning in the ancient game of chaugan, as in the quotation above.

catbird seat, (sitting) in the
To be in a position of advantage or superiority. This expres-sion, originating in the American South, is believed to allude to that loud-mouthed southern bird's unreachable perch high in a tree. It was popularized in the 1940's by Mississippi-born baseball announcer Red Barber, for many years the "voice" of the Brooklyn Dodgers. When it seemed clear that a pitcher was not going to allow any more hits, Barber declared he was now in the catbird seat. The term gained further currency when James Thurber used it as the title of a short story about

a mild-mannered accountant who was so annoyed by a colleague using this and similar terms that he was planning to murder him, and again when Barber became co-author of a 1968 book about baseball called *Rhubarb in the Catbird Seat*. Barber himself said he picked up the term in a poker game in which it was used by a player with a winning hand, but his own use of it made it permanently associated with baseball.

> *"There's catch as catch can, hit or miss, luck is all."*
> —KANE O'HARA, *Midas*, 2:8 (1761)

catch-as-catch-can

Anyhow, by any method, with no specific plan or order. The term comes from a style of wrestling introduced in the late 19th century. Also called *free style*, it is the most popular of three official styles, and it allows contestants to trip, tackle, and use holds against any part of the opponent's body. However, versions of this expression date back as far as the 14th century, and one appeared in a proverb collection of 1545, which had "Catch that catch may." It also is the name of a children's game.

> *"The smaller software producers are constantly playing catch-up with big guys like Lotus."*
> —*Business Briefs*, Nov. 3, 1982

catch-up, to play

To make a special effort to overcome or overtake a competitor. The term comes from sports, where it means to embark on a riskier style or strategy in order to defeat an opponent's overwhelming lead. Perhaps the most dramatic example is when an ice hockey team behind by one or two goals replaces its goaltender with an extra skater in the final minute or two of the game.

caught in a squeeze play: *see* SQUEEZE PLAY.

"My right ear feels like a cauliflower. Does it look rum?"
—P. G. WODEHOUSE, *White Feather* (1907)

cauliflower ear
A disfigured or deformed ear. The term was first used in boxing about the turn of the 20th century for a boxer's ear that
had been so distorted and distended by repeated blows that it
physically resembled the vegetable. It actually results from
hematomas (blood clots) that become calcified and block the
blood supply to the ear cartilage. The same kind of injury can
occur in wrestling. The deformity can be prevented if the
blood clot is promptly removed. The name was later extended
to a similar deformity resulting from injuries from other
causes (such as automobile accidents).

"The king and queen of games [hold] court."
—JOHN ALLAN MAY, *Christian Science Monitor*, June 23, 1986

center court
The center of attention. The term comes from the central
court at Wimbledon, England, where what some consider to
be *the* major tennis tournament of the year is held each June.
In the early rounds, matches take place on a number of courts
simultaneously, but the highest-ranked, most popular players
are usually scheduled to play on the center court (in Britain
spelled *centre court*), which allows for the largest number of
spectators, and the semifinal and final events always take
place there. Tennis competition at Wimbledon began in 1877
with only one event, a men's singles title for which 22 players
competed. Two hundred spectators saw the final match, in
which Spencer W. Gore defeated W. Marshall (6–1, 6–2, 6–4).
From the 1960's on, when Wimbledon was reaching larger and
larger audiences via television, the term "center court" began
to be extended to arenas other than tennis stadiums.

champ, champion

The outstanding individual in any field. Although the word
originated in medieval jousting, which strictly speaking was
not entirely an athletic event, in modern times it gained currency mainly through sports.

As John Ciardi pointed out, medieval law permitted trial
by combat, based on faith in a God who would assure that
might made right. Thus litigants could appoint *champions*,
swordsmen who took the field ("champion" comes from the
Latin *campus*, for "field") on their behalf and in this way decide the outcome of their lawsuit. Another kind of champion
was the Champion of England, or King's Champion, whose job
it was to ride on Coronation Day and challenge any person
who disputed the right of succession. This office was established by William the Conqueror and was passed on through
a single family. The custom of challenge, however, was abandoned with the coronation of King George IV in 1820, after
which the Champion merely carried the sovereign's standard
at a coronation.

Although in modern parlance a champion still is a person
who fights for something or someone, the words *champion*
and *championship* have been associated with the winners of
athletic contests on both sides of the Atlantic since the early
18th century and therefore merit inclusion in this book.
Titleholders in boxing, in particular, are always said to hold
the championship in their division, and today the abbreviation, *champ*, originally coming from mid-19th-century America, is almost exclusively used for titleholders and other
sports winners. "Champion" and "championship" also have
been transferred to many other kinds of "best"—for example,
"the champion new rose of the year" named by the horticul-
tural society—and, in Britain particularly, the terms are used
simply to mean general excellence (as in "a champion restaurant") without having entered any sort of contest.

change of pace

A shift in one's normal routine; a variation in one's normal
activities. This term comes from several sports—racing, base-

ball, tennis—in which altering the speed of something (a horse's pace, a pitched ball, a racket stroke) may figure as part of the strategy. In baseball in particular the term long designated a slow pitch after one or more fast balls, intended to throw off the batter's timing. The term, common from the 1920's on, was replaced in the 1940's by *change-up*, meaning a slow pitch thrown with the same arm and body action as a fast ball, and similarly intended to fool the batter. The transfer to other activities took place in the mid-20th century and involved a slight alteration in meaning. For example, the statement "Mary's decided to stop working on the report and do a little filing, just for a change of pace," simply means the subject is going to vary her work, with no particular intention of deceiving an opponent (or indeed involving an opponent).

charley horse
Muscle pain and stiffness, particularly in the thigh. There are several theories as to the precise origin of this Americanism, but the principal ones all involve sports, and indeed athletes are probably more likely to suffer from the condition than the general population. The most frequently cited origin is the 19th-century practice of using draft horses to drag the baseball infield, and likening the limping of an afflicted player to that of an elderly horse so employed. If this is true, Charley probably was the name of either a horse or a player, but "charley horse" began to be used for muscle aches and pains causing a person to limp from the 1880's on.

John Ciardi theorizes that the expression ultimately may have come from the 19th-century British term "charley horse" for a horse that pulls up lame. This term in turn, Ciardi suggests, was derived from the 18th-century slang word *charley* for a night watchman, often a partially disabled veteran, so called because the practice of giving such jobs to veterans became common during the reign of King Charles II. Logical as it might appear, this derivation seems somewhat far-fetched.

"The fact that the Vice President called the Governor Mario means that the 1992 Presidential race has officially begun. Cheap shots will whiz by like Ping-Pong balls."

—ANNA QUINDLEN, *New York Times,* Nov. 23, 1991

cheap shot

Deliberately rough treatment of an opponent, verbal or physical, when it is not expected. The term comes from contact sports such as football, where it denotes an intentionally rough tackle or block, particularly when the whistle is being or has been blown to stop play. John Madden describes such a play although he discounts it: "As Lynn Swann [Pittsburgh Steelers wide receiver] cut into George [George Atkinson, Raiders safety]'s area, George took a swing at him. To me that was an instinctive reaction by a safety, not a cheap shot" (*Hey, Wait a Minute,* 1984).

"I was one of the three cheerleaders in the Brown game."

—FRANKLIN D. ROOSEVELT, Letter, 1903

cheerleader

A person who encourages others to do their best. The word comes from the person who leads spectators in organized cheering for a team, at pep rallies and games. The practice of cheerleading, and the name for it, come from late 19th-century America, particularly in school and college sports. It began to be transferred to other kinds of encouragement in the mid-20th century, on both sides of the Atlantic. Thus Terrence Rafferty, in a film review in *The New Yorker,* said: "He's a fantastic cheerleader: when he speaks at a union meeting, it turns into something like a high-school pep rally before the big game" (Mar. 23, 1992).

Chinaman's chance: *see* NOT A CHINAMAN'S CHANCE.

*"Pressure does crazy things to athletes. Some love it,
thrive on it. Others choke on it."*
—HERMAN L. MASIN, *Scholastic Coach*, Nov., 1980

choke, to

To become too tense or anxious to perform well in a crucial
situation. This American colloquialism, used at first for athletic performance but later extended to business, military conflict, or any area where one's actions may be critical at some
point, is a figurative allusion to actual choking, or suffocation.
It is also sometimes put as to *choke up;* the British equiva-
lents are to *clutch,* or *clutch up.* See also CLUTCH HITTER.

circus catch

A spectacular, dramatic feat. The term comes from 19th-
century baseball, where it was first used for any particularly
difficult and acrobatic catch, with the player jumping, diving,
or flipping for the ball. It was later transferred to similar
feats—both literal and figurative—in other areas, but is not
widely used.

*"A clay pigeon is better than no pigeon, and who
knows, they might shoot at it."*
—KAREN KIJEWSKI, *Katwalk* (1989)

clay pigeon

A person likely to be taken advantage of; a fall guy. This expression comes from the target used in trapshooting, a sport
devised by hunters when the supply of birds and hunting
grounds in England began to shrink. Originally in this sport,
the gunner placed a live bird under his hat, released it when
a signal was given, put the hat back on, and only then was
permitted to shoot at the bird in flight. As the supply of birds
shrank, their first replacement was a glass ball placed in a cup
with a spring; when the spring was released, the ball "flew"
out. Later a revolving trap was devised, which sent glass balls
in various directions. In the 1860's these devices were replaced by the clay pigeon, a saucer-shaped target made of

baked clay, with a tip of cardboard glued to the edge to cause it to fly in an eccentric fashion, simulating the flight of birds. It was thrown from a spring trap, which had a clamp so fixed that the target could fly only with the edge exposed. However, these pigeons were so hard that gunfire could not break them, and a variety of other materials were tried. A mixture of river silt and pitch proved an ideal combination.

Trapshooting as a sport was introduced to the United States in the late 1870's and became very popular. In trapshooting a single trap is used. In skeet, a form invented in America about 1920, two traps are used and targets are thrown singly or in pairs. Skeet was introduced to Olympic competition in 1968.

The official clay pigeon is black asphalt, weighs 3.5 to 4 ounces (99 to 113 grams), and has a diameter of 4.29 inches (110 millimeters). It emerges from the trap at a speed of approximately 50 miles (80 kilometers) per hour. Competitors use a 12-gauge open-bore shotgun, with an effective maximum range of 40 yards (36.82 meters). The clay pigeon disintegrates when it is hit mainly because it is spinning.

The transfer of the term to figurative use took place in the first half of the 20th century and may be related to the much older use of *pigeon* as a slang term for a dupe. In Britain, bicycle and motorcycle couriers call pedestrians "clay pigeons," for their propensity to knock them down on crowded London streets.

> "*Of course, in the restaurant game the cleanup hitter is the chef.*"
>
> —BRYAN MILLER, *New York Times*, Jan. 31, 1992

cleanup hitter

The most dependable or skillful member of a group; a candidate who can effect a major change in policy, affairs, etc. The term comes from baseball, where it designates the fourth position in the batting order, usually assigned to a powerful hitter. The reason, of course, is that if the first three batters can get on base, the cleanup hitter may be able to drive them and himself home, "cleaning up" or "clearing" the bases and resulting in four runs for the team.

"The 'King' and 'Queen' go into a clinch."
                        —JOHN OSBORNE, *Paul Slickey*, 1:4 (1959)

clinch
Lovers' embrace. This colloquialism dates back to about 1900 and undoubtedly came from the meaning of clinch in boxing, that is, grappling or holding each other about the arms or body in order to hinder or prevent punching. Often it occurs after a vigorous exchange of punches, and it is up to the referee to break up the clinch and keep the fight from stalling. This usage of clinch in boxing has been around since the second half of the 19th century. The word has other meanings as well, but it is the boxing term that was transferred to the lovers' embrace, and indeed, the boxers do look as though they are hugging.

close call, a
A narrow escape. This originally American term dates from the 1880's and probably comes from baseball or another sport, where it described a situation in which an official's decision could have gone either way. Even if it did not originate in baseball, the term continued to have that meaning there. Christy Mathewson described it in his book on pitching (1912): "Most clubs try to keep an umpire from feeling hostile toward the team because, even if he means to see a play right, he is likely to call a close one against his enemies, not intending to be dishonest."

close counts only in horseshoes
To miss by only a little still means to fail. This expression comes from pitching horseshoes, where a side scores three points for a *ringer*—that is, when the horseshoe thrown encircles the stake—but also scores one point when its horseshoe comes closer than one thrown by the immediately preceding opponent. Consequently, coming close counts, although not as much as a completely successful toss. In the late 20th century

the term was occasionally transferred, particularly for predictions and estimates referring to political campaigns, the state of the economy, and the like.

close finish
Uncertain outcome. The term comes from races and other competitive sports where the competitors are so evenly matched and the results are so close that they are difficult to call. See also BLANKET FINISH.

clutch hitter
A person who comes through to save a critical situation. This American slang term comes from baseball, where a *clutch* is a tight situation in which the outcome of a game is at stake. A clutch hitter is a batter who can consistently make a big play in such situations. The term, used in baseball since at least the 1940's, has been transferred to other sports—for example, a *clutch shooter* in basketball—as well as to nonsporting situations. See also CHOKE.

come up smiling, to
To recover cheerfully from adversity. The term originated in the boxing ring of the late 19th century, when it was said of a fighter who got up after having been knocked down and was ready to resume fighting. It soon began to be used figuratively for recovering from other kinds of misfortune. P. G. Wodehouse had it in *If I Were You* (1931): "You come up smiling after having a whacking great car run into you" (cited by *OED*).

> "He came up to the scratch at the moment appointed."
>
> —ANONYMOUS, *John Bull* (1821)

come up to scratch, to
To perform in a satisfactory way. The term comes from boxing, where from the 18th century on *scratch* referred to a line drawn or scratched across the center of the ring. The boxers had to come up to this line to start an encounter. Also, after

a knockdown and thirty-second wait, a fighter had eight seconds to get back to the scratch; if he could not get there without help, he was considered defeated.

However, "scratch" is also used in a more general way to denote a line or mark indicating a starting point or boundary in races and other sports, and it is particularly associated with golf, where it denotes a standard of performance. A *scratch man* is a golfer who is supposed to play to a course's *scratch score*, that is, consistently play equal to or better than the standard scratch score of his own or other courses. He or she is then given a *handicap of scratch*. Also see START FROM SCRATCH.

connect, to

To be truly successful. The term is used in several sports. In boxing it means to land a punch on one's opponent; in baseball it means to hit a pitched ball (sometimes, to hit a homer). It was transferred to other enterprises about the mid-20th century.

> "*I don't punch until the other guy do . . . I'm really a counterpuncher when I go to the body.*"
> —Heavyweight champion JOE FRAZIER

counterpunch, to

To retaliate, rather than to initiate hostilities. The term comes from boxing, where it has two meanings. As described in the quotation above, the counterpuncher specializes in letting the opponent attack first and then hitting back. Counterpunching also means to parry or block an opponent's lead, and answer with a punch. The term was transferred to figurative use about the middle of the 20th century.

> "*The judges were proceeding to 'count out' his antagonist.*"
> —*The Repertory*, Aug. 2, 1808

count out, to
To declare defeated, or eliminated. The term comes from boxing, which has always had some sort of rule whereby a fighter is judged defeated. By today's rules, if he is knocked out for ten seconds, which are literally counted off by the referee, he is out. This ten-second procedure is also known as *the count*.

This usage is not the same as *to count someone out*, which means simply to exclude someone and has no association with sports. Rather, it uses "to count" in the meaning of "to consider," which has also been around since the 19th century. "When it comes to hunting grizzlies on a pony, jist count me out," said a writer in *Knickerbocker Magazine* (June, 1854).

cricket: *see* NOT CRICKET

> *"The story of the curve ball is the story of the game itself. Some would say of life itself."*
> —MARTIN QUIGLEY, *The Curve Ball in American Baseball History* (1984)

curve, (throw) a
A surprise, often but not always an unpleasant one; an unexpected turn of events. The term comes from a basic throw in the baseball pitcher's repertory, a pitch thrown with sufficient downward or sideward spin so as to make it veer from its expected path. A right-handed pitcher's curve ball tends to break toward the left, and a southpaw's toward the right. Alternating curve balls with fast balls and other kinds of pitch is the standard way of trying to fool the batter, who can find them frustrating indeed. "Carrots might be good for my eyes," said Brooklyn Dodger Carl Furillo, "but they won't straighten out the curve ball." The term was transferred to other enterprises by the mid-20th century. "Mr. Zweben's menu combines traditional American fare and colorful contemporary creations, plus a couple of curve balls like duck confit egg rolls," wrote *New York Times* restaurant critic Bryan Miller (Jan. 31, 1992).

"Stranger, pause and shed a tear
For one who leaves no mourners
D. F. Sapp reposes here:
He would cut corners."
                    —ANONYMOUS, Epitaph of Mr. Sapp (c. 1910)

cut corners, to
To take a chance or risk; also, to do a hasty, sloppy job. The
term presumably comes from some kind of race in which a
competitor is rounding turns very closely. It dates from the
early 19th century. John Johnson had a literal description in
The Oriental Voyager (1807): "They make most excellent drivers, and think nothing of turning short corners."

The second meaning derives from the fact that rounding
corners very narrowly shortens the course, which in other
contexts became doing a haphazard job. For example, "He always cut corners in his assignments, generally just reading
the table of contents and skimming through relevant chap-
ters."

D D D D D

daily double

An outside chance; a very long shot. The term refers to a system of betting on a horse race in which one must pick the winners of two stipulated races—usually the first and second—in order to win. The chances of winning therefore are not very great, but the payoff is. The first daily double to pay more than $10,000 was at Washington Park Race Track in Chicago on August 14, 1939, where the horses Joy Bet and Merry Caroline combined to pay $10,772.40. Only one ticket for this bet was sold. The term has signified any kind of long shot since the mid-20th century. In a *Time* interview discussing narcissistic individuals, psychologist Steven Berglas, referring to four pathological traits they exhibit, said, " 'Hitting a quad' in my practice is as rare as winning the daily double at Aqueduct" (Nov. 4, 1991).

daisy-cutter

An antipersonnel fragmentation bomb used in World War II. Dropped by the Japanese from airplanes, it was so rigged that it went off a few feet above the ground and thus "cut daisies" in all directions. The name was coined by American GI's, who may or may not have taken it from much older British usages. Since the 18th century British riders have used it for a horse that does not raise its feet high when trotting, presumably with the thought that its feet cut off the heads of daisies. This usage also crossed the Atlantic. Washington Irving had it in a letter of 1847: "My horse now and then cuts daisies with me when I am on his back." By the mid-19th century the term was also used in cricket, and soon afterward in baseball, for a ball that was either bowled or batted very low, just skimming the ground. Mark Twain had it in *A Connecticut Yankee at King Arthur's Court* (1889): "I've seen him catch a daisy-cutter in his teeth."

dark horse

A candidate who unexpectedly becomes a successful contender. The term was first used in horse racing for an unknown horse about whose qualities nothing was known. It
appears in an 1831 novel, *The Young Duke*, by Benjamin
Disraeli: "... and a dark horse which had never been thought
of ... rushed past the grand stand in sweeping triumph."
However, it was in America that it was first transferred to
political candidates, specifically James Polk, who in 1844 was
nominated on the Democratic Party's eighth ballot although
he had not even been mentioned as a candidate until then, and
who won the election, becoming eleventh President of the
United States.

dash, hundred-yard

A brief spell of great activity. The term, an early 19th-century
Americanism, comes from a short race in track and field
events, in which the runner goes at full speed for the entire
distance. In the 20th century it was transferred to other enterprises, as in "Forty guests were arriving at eight o'clock,
and the groceries hadn't even been delivered; for the third
time that week the kitchen staff was preparing for a hundred-
yard dash."

dead heat

A tie; a contest in which the competitors are exactly equal
and no one has won. The term comes from 18th-century British horse racing and is still used in racing of various kinds on
both sides of the Atlantic. Moreover, since cameras were introduced to photograph the finish of races, the occurrence of
a dead heat has become much more common, not only in horse
racing but in track and field as well. A famous dead-heat photograph was taken in the United States Olympic trials at Los
Angeles in 1952, in which two runners were declared tied for
third place in the 100-meter dash. This was the first official
dead heat called in track, and as a result both runners, Jim
Gathers and Dean Smith, qualified to race in the Olympic
Games in Helsinki. (See also PHOTOFINISH.) The word *heat*

means one round in a race that will be decided by winning two or more *trials*. In such races betting may take place on each individual heat, as well as on the outcome of the race. The term was transferred to other kinds of competition in the 20th century, as in "The Big Three auto manufacturers were in a dead heat in getting their new models to the dealers."

deck, to

To knock down. This 20th-century American colloquialism appears to have originated in boxing, where "deck" may refer to the canvas-covered floor of the boxing ring. In the second half of the 20th century it began to be used in football as well, as in "Unitas was decked after he let the ball go." It then became a general term for being knocked down, whatever the cause or source, but only in informal speech.

> *"I want you, besides, to act as decoy in a case I have already told you of."*
>
> —CHARLES DICKENS, *Martin Chuzzlewit* (1843)

decoy

A lure to entice or entrap someone. The term comes from hunting water fowl, where an imitation bird carved out of wood or some other material is placed in a body of water in order to attract live birds. The word "decoy" has been used both for this practice and for the place where it was carried out since at least the early 17th century; for a time the word *decoy-duck* also was used, since ducks are the principal quarry in such hunting. By the 1630's the term also was being used figuratively for a person who entices or allures someone into some kind of trap.

designated hitter

Also, *DH*. A person who steps in to help out, in either an emergency or a case of unexpected need. The term comes from baseball, where it means a player who is picked before the game begins to bat for the pitcher(s) but who does not play a field position in that game. Since 1973 the American League has permitted this use of a tenth player anywhere in the batting order. For a time the player was also known as a *designated pinch-hitter*, but this terminology was dropped. The transfer to other areas, in which designated hitter means much the same as "substitute," occurred almost immediately and has remained current, as in "Joe stepped in as designated hitter when the regular announcer got stuck in a snowstorm and couldn't get to the studio."

Dick Smith

A person who drinks alone or, if he is with others, never treats them to drinks. The term was first used in the 1870's for a baseball player who habitually kept to himself and was known as something of a tightwad. Its source has been lost—no one remembers if there actually was a person with this name—but it is not often heard today and may be obsolescent, if not obsolete.

> *"The beautiful but pernicious game of billiards."*
> —JOHN WILSON, *Noctes Ambrosianae* (1827)

dirty pool

Unfair or unethical behavior. This American colloquialism refers to cheating at pool, which, as John Ciardi pointed out, is fairly difficult to do. Pool tends to be aboveboard, and watchful players can readily spot anyone who moves the cue ball or manipulates the object balls. Nevertheless, the term entered the language and was transferred to any kind of dishonesty. Herman Wouk had it in *The Caine Mutiny* (1951): "I played pretty dirty pool, you know, in court."

> *"You had to keep those guys from falling asleep, because I've seen guys fall right off that bench and onto the disabled list."*
> —All-Star pitcher BOB FELLER

disabled list, on the

Out of commission; unable to perform. The term originated in baseball, where it is used for an injured player who is still on the roster but may not play for 15 or 21 days. During this period the team may add another player as a temporary replacement, who is retired when the injured player returns. The expression began to be used figuratively for ailing employees, broken machinery, and the like during the second half of the 20th century, as in "MGM Pathé Communications and the bankrupt Orion Pictures Corporation are both on Tinseltown's disabled list" (*New York Times*, May 17, 1992).

Don't look back, something might be gaining on you

Don't worry about the past and do your best now, lest someone surpass you. This oft-repeated statement was one of a set of "rules" pitcher Leroy ("Satchel") Paige (1906–1982) developed as answers when sportswriters asked him how he stayed so young. In 1948, after a twenty-year career in organized baseball, Paige, who was black, joined the Cleveland Indians as a rookie pitcher. The oldest rookie in major-league history, he was selected Rookie of the Year. He was famous for his unusual windup and extraordinary fastball, and he continued to play on major-league teams until 1965. In 1971 he was inducted into the Baseball Hall of Fame. Other bits of his folk wisdom were to avoid eating fried meat and to avoid running at all times.

> *"The only thing worse than a Mets game is a Mets doubleheader."*
>
> —New York Yankees Manager CASEY STENGEL
> (attributed in early 1960's)

doubleheader

Two events that take place in immediate succession or within a short time of each other. This expression was transferred to other events from baseball, although it was used even earlier for a railroad train pulled by two locomotives. The latter use has long been forgotten, and the term became indelibly associated with baseball, where it means two consecutive games played by the same teams in one day, for which spectators pay only a single admission. The earliest such occurrence in the major leagues was on September 25, 1882, when two National League teams, Worcester and Providence, played back-to-back games. The first American League doubleheader took place on July 15, 1901, between Baltimore and Washington. In both instances the results were split, each team winning one game. Baseball doubleheaders frequently are played in order to make up a postponed game.

A basketball doubleheader, in contrast, may be two games played by different pairs of teams. In automobile racing, the two races may take place on consecutive days, but spectators still pay a single admission price.

When transferred, a single price of admission is not necessarily part of the term. Thus, in "We took in a doubleheader at the Metropolitan Opera—*Aïda* in the afternoon and *Carmen* that same evening," it is safe to assume the speaker bought tickets for each performance.

double play

Two simultaneous accomplishments. The term comes from baseball, where it signifies putting out two players on a single pitch. A double play can occur in several ways: A batter may hit a fly that is caught and puts out a base runner before he can advance or retreat to a base; a batter may strike out and the catcher may throw out a runner trying to steal a base; or two runners may be forced out on a ball thrown first to one base and then another. The term began to be used in baseball in the 1860's but was not transferred to other affairs until the 20th century, as in "Our attorney made a brilliant double play, not only winning the case but establishing an important legal precedent."

> "*I'm the janitor and corresponding secretary of the Down-and-Out Club.*"
>
> —O. HENRY, *No Story* (1909)

down and out

Penniless and without any resources. This term originated in boxing, where it denotes being knocked down and staying down for at least ten seconds, consequently losing the bout. This situation is also described as *taking the (full) count* or being *out for the count* (see also COUNT OUT). Being down and out was transferred to other kinds of loser by the early 20th century. (See also DOWN BUT NOT OUT.)

Interestingly, the same term means something quite different in another sport. In football, it is a pass pattern where the receiver runs straight down the field and then cuts sharply to the outside; it is usually employed after a fake.

> *"A man may be down, but he's never out."*
> —E. C. LEFFINGWELL, *Slogan of the Salvation Army* (coined c. 1925)

down but not out
Temporarily set back but still to be reckoned with. In prize-fighting, a fighter who is knocked down must stay down for a specified period of time before being deemed the loser; he thus is said to be *down for the count*. (See also DOWN AND OUT.)

down to the wire
To the last minute; to the very end. The term comes from horse racing, where it long was the practice to extend a wire across and above the track at the finish line of the course. It was transferred to situations other than racing about the turn of the 20th century. A 1950 newspaper item had it, "Baseball season is coming down to the wire" (*Keowee Courier;* cited by *OED*). Also see UNDER THE WIRE.

drop one's guard, to
To abandon one's defenses; to become unprotected. Although the companion phrase, *on one's guard*, is much older and comes from warfare, the current term is derived from boxing, where one literally puts up one's fist to guard against the opponent's blows. It is usually the fighter's lower hand that guards the chin (the right hand in right-handed individuals, the left in southpaws). Lowering (dropping) it leaves the chin

vulnerable. On losing to Gene Tunney in 1926, prizefighter Jack Dempsey told his wife, "Honey, I forgot to duck."

drop the ball, to

To make a mistake; to miss an opportunity. This term is used in a number of sports. Chief among them are football, where it is applied to either a player carrying the ball or a receiver who fails to catch a pass (see also FUMBLE ON THE PLAY), and baseball, where it is applied to a fielder failing to catch a fly. The term has been applied to more general kinds of mistake since about 1950. For example, the *Boston Globe* caption under a news photo read, "The US Marine Corps color guard drops the ball with its presentation of the Canadian flag last night." Ironically, this mistaken display, in which the Canadian flag with its maple leaf was held upside down, occurred at the second 1992 World Series game between the Atlanta Braves and Toronto Blue Jays, the first Series ever in which a Canadian team played.

In golf the term has a totally different meaning, that is, substituting another ball for a lost one, or putting in play a ball that has gone out of bounds or is in an unplayable lie. In these situations the player drops the replacement ball backward over his or her shoulder.

dunk shot

A forceful attempt to achieve something. The term comes from basketball, where it means jumping in the air and pushing the ball into the basket from above the basket rim, using one or both hands. (The sports terminology itself probably comes from the older meaning of dunking, that is, dipping something into liquid, such as dunking doughnuts into coffee.) See also SLAM DUNK.

E   E   E   E   E

"[Cricket] A game the British, not being a spiritual people, had to invent in order to have some conception of eternity."

—Attributed to LORD BANCROFT

early innings, it's

It's only the first part of a course of events, with the implication that a great deal more can happen. The term comes from cricket, where an *innings* (always used in this plural form) is a turn at bat, either for an individual batsman or a team. For a batsman it continues until he is "out." For a team, it continues until ten players are declared "out" or the captain declares the innings closed (because he believes the team has scored enough runs to win). Unlike baseball, where the average game consists of nine innings and an inning normally continues for no more than half an hour (and often much less), a major cricket match usually consists of just two innings for each team and is played over two to three days. Given this length of time, "early innings" takes on considerable temporal significance. Roger Angell used it as the title of an autobiographical piece concerning his early boyhood interest in baseball (*The New Yorker*, February, 1992).

easy out, an

Anyone or anything that can be dealt with effortlessly. The expression comes from baseball, where it is said of a weak batter, especially a pitcher, who can be struck out with relative ease. In amateur games such as Little League, the term is used as a taunting shout intended to rattle the batter.

end run
An attempt to avoid something or someone. The term comes
from football, where it denotes an offensive play in which the
ball-carrier runs around one end of the line of scrimmage. It
was transferred to other kinds of evasive action by the second
half of the 20th century, as in "But in what amounts to an end
run around the scholarly blockade, two researchers ... devised a computer program that used a listing of all the words
in one collection of scrolls to reconstruct part of the original
text" (John Noble Wilford, writing about a bootleg version of
the Dead Sea Scrolls, *New York Times*, Sept. 5, 1991).

end zone
The point of summing up or completion. The term comes from
football, where it signifies a ten-yard-deep area (in Canadian
football, a twenty-yard-deep area) at either end of the field
bounded by goal line, end line, and sidelines. The only way to
score a touchdown is to get the ball in the other team's end
zone, either by moving it there or by gaining possession of it

there. The term "end zone" figures in other sports, too. In ice hockey it is a zone at either end of the rink extending from the closest blue line to the goal line, and it similarly constitutes an area of attack and defense; this area is also called *inside the blue line, the team's end,* or simply *the zone.* (The hockey rink is divided into three equal zones by two blue lines that run parallel to the goal lines.) In lacrosse it is the playing area at either end of the field behind the goals.

The transferred meaning of "end zone," however, appears to come mainly from American football. Doris Grumbach used it in the title of her memoir, *Coming into the End Zone* (1991).

enter the arena, to
To compete (in politics, business, etc.). The term, which is derived from the gladiatorial arena of ancient Rome, refers to the playing field of modern-day sports. It has long been transferred to other competitive enterprises, as in "With the primaries only weeks away, numerous contenders for state office are entering the arena."

extra innings
Additional time allowed for completing a project. The term comes from baseball, where a game normally consists of nine innings, in each of which both teams have a turn at bat (offense) and in the field (defense). If the score is tied at the end of nine innings, play continues for as many extra innings as needed to break the tie.

F F F F F

face-off, a
An open confrontation, signaling the start of hostilities or
competition. The term comes from ice hockey, where at the
beginning or resumption (after a stoppage) of play the referee
or linesman drops the puck on the ice between two opposing
players, who are lined up face to face. Each tries to get control of the puck. Lacrosse also begins with a face-off. The center attackers from each team crouch opposite each other at
midfield, the ball is placed between their sticks, and at a signal they struggle for possession of the ball or a chance to pass
it to a teammate. The expression was transferred to other
areas from the mid-20th century on, as in "Diplomacy is the
art of avoiding a face-off whenever possible."

"They were indeed fair game for the laughers."
—THOMAS MACAULAY, *Essays: Milton* (1825)

fair game
A legitimate object of attack. The expression originated in
hunting. The word *game* itself was transferred to figurative
use—that is, an object of pursuit—by the 17th century. By the
early 19th century the idea of legitimate pursuit had been
transferred, so that Maria Edgeworth had it in *Belinda*
(1801): "Quiz the doctor . . . he's an author, so fair game." More
recently, a *Boston Globe* headline concerning the firing of Boston Bruins coach Rick Bownes was "Coach Is Fair Game in an
Unfair Business" (June 9, 1992). See also OPEN SEASON ON.

"She endeavoured . . . to give both sides fair play."
—CHARLES JENNER, *The Placid Man* (1770)

fair play

Upright conduct, just treatment, honorable behavior. This term seems to have antedated its use and references in athletics. Shakespeare already had it in *King John:* "Shall we upon the footing of our land send fayre-play-orders, and make compromise" (5:1). But just a few years later Fletcher and Massinger, in their play *The Custom of the Country* (1619), used the term with a specific allusion to games: "Fair play, and above-board, too." In the 19th century the idea of fairness in playing various sports cropped up again and again, although "fair" here sometimes took on the meaning of legitimate according to the rules—for example, a *fair ball* as opposed to a foul ball. See also PLAY FAIR.

fake out, to

To deceive an opponent. Although "to fake" in the sense of "to pretend" has been around much longer, this 20th-century American slang expression comes from football. Time-honored football plays include pretending to pass or kick when not actually doing so, and moving in one direction when one is really heading the opposite way, always with the object of fooling the opposing team. Such feints are also very important in basketball, and occasionally occur in ice hockey and baseball (for example, a fake pick-off attempt). They may even figure in tennis, where a prime example was Michael Chang's sudden underhand serve to Ivan Lendl in the semifinals of the 1989 French Open.

The term was transferred to more general forms of deception in the second half of the 20th century.

fall short (of the mark), to

To be insufficient; to fail to reach. This term comes from such sports as archery and horseshoes, where an arrow or horseshoe drops to the ground before reaching the target. The term was being transferred to other kinds of failure (or *short-*

fall) by the late 16th century. Edmund Spenser had it in *The Faerie Queene* (1596): "They fall too short of our fraile reckoning."

"Making four false starts."
—F. E. SMEDLEY, *Frank Fairlegh* (1850)

false start, a

A premature or unsuccessful beginning. This term comes from various kinds of race in which a competitor moves across the starting line before the signal has been given. Too many false starts can lead to being disqualified—two are allowed in track events, and either two or three in swimming races. The term is also used in football for a move by an offensive player after he has assumed the set position but before the ball is snapped; there it calls for a five-yard penalty for that player's team.

"Fans don't boo nobodies."
—REGGIE JACKSON, controversial
Oakland A's slugger in the 1970's

fan

An outspoken supporter or loyal follower of something or someone. There are at least two theories about the origin of this term. One holds that it was first used in boxing in Britain in the early 1800's. Boxing then was a popular spectator sport for the gentry, who would drive to boxing matches in their carriages, dressed in their accustomed finery. The boxers and their promoters, who came from a quite different social class, described these spectators as "fancy," which was later shortened to "fance" and eventually to "fan." Another theory, subscribed to by the etymologists of the *OED*, holds the word to be a shortening of "fanatic," meaning a wild enthusiast. At any rate, the word came into widespread use in the late 19th century for ardent sports enthusiasts, especially in baseball. The term was used in Kansas in the late 19th century for baseball fans and had spread as far west as Oregon by 1919.

By then it was well known on both sides of the Atlantic and was applied also to film and theater enthusiasts (who later gave rise to *fan clubs*, whose members are devoted to one or another actor or actress and deluge them with *fan letters* or *fan mail*).

fancy Dan

A dandy; a showy but ineffective individual. The term originated in American sports, where it was used for a person with a flashy style and/or appearance but poor in performance. As heavyweight Jack Dempsey put it in his 1950 book, *Championship Fighting*, "The amateur and professional ranks today are cluttered with 'fancy Dans.'"

fancy footwork

Skillful maneuvering in any situation. The term can be used in numerous sports but probably originated in boxing. Fighters move their feet both to maneuver in relation to their opponent and to make sure they have the best possible balance and leverage for punching. The term was later extended to any kind of adroit moves to improve one's own position, as in "It took some fancy footwork for the candidate to avoid these personal questions."

fanny pack

A zippered pouchlike container that is worn around the waist. This contraption and its name come from cross-country skiing, for which it was invented about 1970. In it a skier could carry goggles, money, a snack, and similar small items in a pack that left the hands free but was less cumbersome than a hiker's knapsack. The name comes from the fact that it was worn with the pouch in back, above the hips—that is, over the "fanny," or backside. (In Britain, however, "fanny" is rude slang for the female genitals, so this name is not used.) In the next couple of decades fanny packs were adopted by more and more nonskiers, at first mainly women who used them instead of a pocketbook but later also men. These users frequently turned them around so that the pouch was in front, making the contents more accessible, but the name "fanny pack" persisted.

> "*Great players beat great defense to make great shots. There were textbook fast breaks.*"
> —BOB RYAN, *Boston Globe,* May 6, 1992

fast break
A quickly executed action. The term comes from basketball, where it describes a play in which the ball is rapidly moved from one end of the court to the other, usually by means of one or two passes, to enable the offensive team to score before the defense can get into position. Used in basketball since the 1940's, the term began to be transferred to other enterprises in the late 20th century.

featherweight
An insignificant person or object. The term comes from boxing, where for a long time it was the lightest weight division, not over 126 pounds in professional boxing and not over 125 pounds in amateur events. The first featherweight boxing champion was "Belfast Spider" Ike Weir, who fought in the 1880's. In the following decade the leading featherweight was George Dixon. Today there are two lighter weight classes, bantamweight (not over 118 pounds) and flyweight (not over 112 pounds). In weightlifting, featherweight refers to a weight of 60 kilograms (132.25 pounds). By the mid-19th century the term was being used figuratively for unimportant persons or objects, as in Annie Edwards's *A Girton Girl* (1885): "It would do your cousin a vast deal of good to run away from that feather-weight husband of hers."

fencing
Giving evasive answers; hedging. This term is a transfer from the sport of two opponents engaging in combat with blunted swords, in which each tries to attack the other and parry the other's attacks. The figurative use of the word alludes to the

large role that parrying plays in this sport and dates from the 17th century and remains current, as in " 'Throughout our first interview she was fencing with me,' the reporter complained." See also PARRY.

field, to
To handle successfully. This usage comes from baseball and cricket, where fielding is the act of catching or picking up a batted ball and, usually, attempting to put out a runner or batsman. From this the term was transferred to more general usage, as in "He's an expert at fielding awkward questions."

fielder's choice
Opportunity to choose between two ways of reaching the same goal. The term comes from baseball, where it describes a situation in which the fielder who has caught the ball may decide which of two runners he will put out, either the batter who is trying to reach first base or some other runner. If he chooses the latter alternative, the batter, who is therefore safe on base, is not credited with a base hit but is charged with a time at bat. In baseball the term dates from the early 1900's. It began to be transferred to other situations in the latter part of the 20th century, as in "Janet can either decline the invitation or show up for the party a day late—fielder's choice."

fill the gap, to
To substitute for or replace another person. The term comes from football. When an offensive lineman moves out of the line of scrimmage to lead interference on a running play, one of his teammates must fill the gap the lineman left. The term began to be used figuratively late in the 20th century.

finish in/out of the money: *see under* MONEY.

finish line
The ultimate goal. The term refers to a line, either actual or imaginary, that marks the end point of a race. It is occasionally used figuratively, as in "She still has all the seams to stitch; she's nowhere near the finish line."

"In two years he hadn't been able to get to first base."
—JOHN AUGUST, *The Woman in the Picture* (1944)

first base, get to
To succeed in the initial phase of an undertaking. The term comes from baseball, where getting to first base by hitting the pitched ball, by being "walked" (being pitched four balls out of the strike zone), or by being hit by a pitched ball (accidentally) is the first step toward scoring a run for the batter's team. By the early 1900's this term had been transferred to taking a first step toward success in any activity. In the mid-20th century the term took on a secondary meaning among teenagers, that is, first base represented the initial stage of sexual intimacy, specifically meaning kissing.

first string
The best or highest-rated members of a group. The term originated in football, where it denotes the players who regularly start or play, as opposed to those held in reserve or as substitutes. It is now used in most team sports, including basketball, baseball, and volleyball. See also A TEAM.

*"He courts me a good deal, and fishes. I fish in return;
and I think that neither of us meets with much luck."*
—THOMAS HUTCHINSON, *Diary*, Oct. 10, 1774

fish, to
To seek indirectly while disguising one's intentions, especially looking for compliments, information, etc. This transfer from the sport of angling has been around since the 17th century or so. See also FISHING EXPEDITION.

*"An admirable knack of fishing out the secrets of his
customers."*
—JOSEPH ADDISON, *The Guardian*, 1713

fishing expedition
Gathering of information without any clearly defined method or end in the hope of discovering something useful. Attorneys

embark on such expeditions by questioning an adversary or examining an adversary's property in order to discover evidence relevant to a case. Because it is controversial—obviously the adversary would oppose it—in the United States the extent of such investigations is governed by federal rules, and the person being investigated may seek a protective order to limit the process. The term, which transfers a literal hunt for fish or fishing grounds to poking into human affairs, has been around since about 1960.

> *"The gods do not deduct from man's allotted span the hours spent in fishing."*
> —Babylonian proverb, often quoted by
> President Herbert Hoover

fish or cut bait

Either get on with it or give up and let someone else have a turn; stop delaying. This imperative exhorting the fisherman who takes up space or a rod or a boat without actually fishing to get on with his task, or at least prepare bait for others, began to be used figuratively in the late 19th century. The *Congressional Record* of 1876 reports that Joseph G. Cannon used the term in a congressional debate, and it was repeated six years later by another congressman.

> *"Oh, give me grace to catch a fish*
> *So big that even I*
> *When talking of it afterwards*
> *May have no need to lie."*
> —ANONYMOUS, *A Fisherman's Prayer*

fish story

A gross exaggeration. "Fishermen are born honest, but they get over it," said octogenarian sports columnist Ed Zern in a *New York Times* interview (Mar. 13, 1992). Indeed, their prevaricating has been taken for granted for at least two hundred years, the length of time that their storytelling ability was extended to mean a tall tale on any subject.

"I was winning the game of life, but there was a flag on the play."

—GORDON GOSS and VALERIE THORNTON, eds.,
Overheard at the Square Dance (1988)

flag on the play

An unforeseen difficulty or setback. The term comes from football, where an official will throw up a flag to signal an infraction of the rules or a foul that will earn a penalty. The flag actually is a bright-colored kerchief (yellow in the NFL), weighted at one end. The term began to be used figuratively in the second half of the 20th century, as in "The officer caught Mary making an illegal U-turn—flag on the play."

flake, flaky

Odd, eccentric. The precise origin of this usage is obscure. However, Tim Considine, in *The Language of Sports*, maintains that it was first applied to San Francisco Giants outfielder Jackie Brandt in the 1950's, which gives the term a rightful place in this book. The *OED* says only that it is originally American slang. However, its first citation, from a *New York Times* article of 1964, says: "flake ... is an insider's word used throughout baseball," and goes on to define it as not quite crazy but, as a later generation might put it, "far out." It has been liberally applied beyond the field of sports to any person who fits this description. See also the near synonym SCREWBALL.

flat-footed, to catch/be caught

To catch or be caught unready. This expression, around since about 1900 in this meaning, is believed to come from baseball, but it might equally well come from some other sport in which a player should literally be on his or her toes, in a "ready" position (see also ON ONE'S TOES). In early 19th-century America, however, to be flat-footed meant to be positive and uncompromising, as in "I stand flat-footed, square-toed, hump-shouldered, upon the platform of free rights and true republicanism" (*Knickerbocker Magazine*, 1854).

flat-out
With maximum effort. This term comes from racing, where competitors in various kinds of race (horse, bicycle, etc.) lean forward, in effect flattening themselves so as to reduce wind resistance and move as fast as possible. Dating from about 1920, the sports term soon was transferred to other kinds of extreme effort.

flooding the zone
Overwhelming the competition. The term comes from football, where, to confuse the defense, the offensive team will send two, three, or four potential pass receivers to the same side of the field. Consequently there are more possible receivers than defensive players in that area. In the second half of the 20th century the term was used figuratively in other enterprises where a similar tactic was employed. For example, "In one attack near Baghdad the Allies were flooding the zone with tanks."

floored, to be
To be overcome, with surprise, confusion, or some other emotion. The term probably comes from boxing, where it means to be literally brought to the floor, but it has the same meaning in riding (a floored horseman is one who has fallen to the ground), wrestling, and other sports. Its figurative use dates from about 1800.

flying start
A very enthusiastic beginning. This term was first used in racing, where it actually meant that an entrant began to move before reaching the starting line. Thus, by the time the boat (or runner, or bicycle, or whatever) reached the starting line, it was moving at full speed. The term was so used in the late 19th century, and by 1930 or so was being used figuratively, as in "John's summer-school course gave him a flying start in picking up colloquial Spanish." Also see RUNNING START.

"Some people think football is a matter of life and death. . . . I can assure them it is much more serious than that."
　　—Attributed to BILL SHANKLY, British football manager (1973)

football, a (political)

An issue or person that is roughly tossed back and forth. The term, of course, refers to the ball used in football, in which the team that gains possession of it and carries it over the goal line most often will win the game. Actually, the seemingly modern figurative use of "football" is extremely old. The *Epistles* of Sextus Aurelius Victor, dating from about A.D. 358, mention "the football of fortune."

　　In recent times the word has acquired yet another, more sinister meaning. Accompanying U.S. President George Bush to a summit meeting in 1990 was an army officer carrying a black case attached to his arm by a chain. According to the *Boston Globe* (Nov. 20, 1990), the bag, called *the football*, contained communications equipment and the secret codes with which the President could order an instant nuclear strike, and accompanied him whenever he was out of the White House. With the breakup of the Soviet Union in 1991, there was some question as to who now held its *nuclear football*. According to *Time* (May 4, 1992), there were three such devices, one held by the Russian president, another by the defense minister, and a third by the Defense Ministry that could replace either of the other two.

"For nearly 20 years, Joe Namath's life revolved around his old knees. His football knees. He needed four operations, two on each knee. . . . But now . . . he has new knees, one of 130,000 Americans who will undergo such surgery this year."
　　—DAVE ANDERSON, *New York Times*, May 3, 1992

football knee

Cartilage and ligament damage to the knee. The malady is so named because it is a common form of injury in football players. New York Jets quarterback Joe Namath began suffering from football knee during his senior year at the University of Alabama and had his first knee operation shortly afterward, when he signed his first Jets contract. The orthopedist, he later said, gave him no more than four years of football. He went on to play twelve seasons with the Jets and one with the Los Angeles Rams but later said he played every single down in pain. Years after his retirement Namath, whom the legendary Paul (Bear) Bryant once called the best athlete he had ever coached, finally received metal-and-plastic replacements for both knees. Other sports and activities cause similar damage (see also RUNNER'S KNEE), but the name of the condition reflects the severe and frequent knee injuries incurred by football players in particular.

foot in the bucket, to have one's
To behave timidly. The term comes from baseball, where it is used in two ways. One is for an unorthodox batter's stance, with the front foot pulled back toward the foul line instead of being pointed at the pitcher. According to Paul Dickson, it is derived from the fact that the old-time foul line was in the direction of the water bucket in the dugout, at one time the only source of refreshments. The second meaning of the term is that the batter pulls away from the plate as he swings, presumably a reflex protective action. It is this sense that has been transferred to other activities, as, for example, "Marie has her foot in the bucket, ready to withdraw from the candidacy."

footwork: *see* FANCY FOOTWORK

forward pass
A major step toward one's ultimate goal. The term comes from football, where it constitutes an important offensive play. The ball is thrown to a receiver who is in front of the passer and who then advances as far as possible toward the opponents' goal. The forward pass only became legal in 1906, the same year in which the flying wedge—an overpowering

tactic that often resulted in serious injury—was outlawed. Only one forward pass is permitted in each down, it may be thrown only to one of five designated offensive players, and it may not be attempted after the ball has advanced beyond the line of scrimmage. Its inclusion represented a major change in the game, since it enabled much smaller players to win. It did not become widespread practice until 1913, in the Notre Dame–Army game, in which quarterback Gus Dorais threw successful forward passes to Knute Rockne. It was Rockne, as head coach of Notre Dame from 1918 to 1931, who consolidated the importance of the forward pass.

foul ball

An ignorant oaf who oversteps the bounds of decency. In baseball a foul ball is simply one that is hit outside the legal limits, called the *foul lines*. The term, in use since the 1860's, has no connotation of personal wrongdoing, but simply counts as a mistake. Similarly, *to foul out* in baseball simply means to be put out because an opponent has caught one's foul ball on the fly. In basketball, however, the same term means to be put out of the game because one has committed too many fouls, or violations of the rules, which may indeed involve malice (deliberately hurting an opponent, for example). Although the figurative foul ball originated in baseball, the transfer added pejorative meaning to the term, which has been so used since the 1920's. Thus calling someone a foul ball is far from a compliment. See also FOUL OFF.

foul off, to

To screw up, to make a mistake. In baseball, where this expression originated, to foul off simply means to hit a foul ball, a mistake that is not particularly serious unless the ball is caught on the fly by an opponent (see under FOUL BALL), in which case the batter is out. However, a batter with two strikes can hit as many uncatchable foul balls as he or she wishes without being penalized for it, since a foul ball never counts as a third strike. In fact, deliberately fouling off pitches is a time-honored technique for irritating and/or tiring out a pitcher. In the annals of baseball history, Chicago White Sox shortstop Luke Appling was an acknowledged expert at this practice. In a 1940 game against the New York Yankees, he fouled off 24 pitches in a single time at bat, trying to wear out the starting pitcher, Red Ruffing. In a game three years later against the Detroit Tigers, Appling fouled off 14 consecutive pitches, so enraging pitcher Dizzy Trout that he next pitched his glove instead of the ball.

Nevertheless, with the transfer of this term to other activities, a more negative connotation evolved, so that in effect fouling off came to be a virtual synonym for "to foul up," that is, to bungle.

.400 hitter

A synonym for HEAVY HITTER. The last to accomplish this average in baseball was Ted Williams of the Boston Red Sox, who hit .406 in 1941 (see BATTING AVERAGE for numerical explanation).

> *"Democratic Free-for-All"*
> —Headline, *New York Times,* Feb. 27, 1992

free-for-all

Up for grabs, open to anyone; also, a fight or contest without rules. This late 19th-century Americanism appears to have originated in horse racing, where it meant a race open to all entrants regardless of age or other qualifications. By the early 1900's it had been extended to mean a fight in which there were no limiting rules (on gouging, biting, and other normally illegal tactics). Somewhat later it came to be used for any enterprise open to all participants who could compete without restriction. This, of course, is the sense of the *Times* headline quoted above, which appeared over an article maintaining that the Democratic presidential nomination was up for grabs.

"In a freewheeling music such as jazz . . ."
—M. STEARNS, *The Story of Jazz* (1957)

freewheeling
Unrestrained, independent, coasting along; also, irresponsible. This term comes from bicycling, where in the late 19th century it was used to describe a bicycle with the rear wheel so arranged that it could rotate while the pedals remained stationary. The term was quickly transferred to other machines—propellers, lawnmowers, etc. However, by 1911 it was being used figuratively as well.

from pillar to post
Here and there; from one place to another. This expression, which originated in the 15th century as *from post to pillar*, is believed to have come from the game of court tennis, the ancestor of modern tennis. The rules in court tennis were quite loose, and so the term alludes to banging about the ball every which way. Another theory holds that the term originally referred to the whipping post and pillory. This origin would better account for the original order but would preclude including the term in this book.

from start to finish
From beginning to end. This particular expression appears to come from 19th-century rowing races, and is used in other sports as well, especially in Britain.

from the word go
From the very beginning. The "go" in this 19th-century Americanism originally meant the start of a race and was transferred to the beginning of any undertaking early in its life. Davy Crockett used it figuratively in his memoirs (1834), and it still tends to be heard more often in America than in Britain.

front runner
The apparent leader in any contest. This 20th-century term comes from racing, where it refers to the leading contender in

a race. Some authorities believe it also carries the connotation of a competitor who performs best when in the lead and setting the pace as opposed to catching up and passing others. However, when this term began to be transferred to other enterprises, particularly to political candidates about 1950, it was applied principally to a candidate who was expected to win. In the 1980's *front-running* came to be used in another sense in the financial world, to describe brokers who executed their own security trades before those of their customers, a practice that is both unethical and illegal.

full count, the
Last chance. The term is used in several sports. In boxing it means that the referee has counted off ten seconds, signifying a knockout and the fight's end. In baseball it signifies a count of three balls and two strikes on the batter; on the next pitched ball he will either walk to first base or will strike out (unless he hits a foul; see FOUL OFF). In bowling the expression signifies a strike on the last ball of a game. However, the figurative usage most likely came from boxing.

full-court press
Out-and-out harassment and disruption. The term comes from a basketball tactic in which the defenders exert pressure on the opposing team over the full length of the court, attempting to disrupt their dribbling and passing so as to regain possession of the ball. In the late 20th century the term began to be used figuratively for other all-out efforts at disruption. During the Gulf War of 1991 the Bush administration used it to signify a major offensive.

fumble on the play
A clumsy error. The term comes from football, where it means accidentally dropping or losing control or possession of the ball when handling or running with it (as opposed to failing to catch a passed or kicked ball). Although this can occur when the ball-carrier is being tackled hard or an opponent snatches the ball away from him, as well as when it simply slips out of

his hands, it is the last sense that has been transferred to other activities. In professional football a fumbled ball becomes a free ball—that is, any player who recovers it may advance it. In his book *Hey, Wait a Minute* (1984), John Madden describes a particularly important fumble that occurred in the 1977 AFC championship game between the Oakland Raiders and Denver Broncos. Bronco Rob Lytle fumbled at the Raiders' one-yard line. Raider Jack Tatum recovered the fumble, and the Broncos scored a touchdown on the next play, for a 14–3 lead. By the rules, it should have been the Raiders' ball fumble, but the head linesman saw neither the fumble nor the recovery and miscalled it.

game, to be

To be spirited, brave, and daring. The term comes from cock-fighting and alludes to the fighting spirit of the game cock. It was transferred to human beings by the early 18th century and is still so used today, although it may also have the somewhat milder meaning of being willing to attempt something, as in "If you want to drive five hundred miles every day, I'm game."

game isn't/ain't over till it's over: *see* IT AIN'T . . .

> *"Some people talk about a game plan like it was a document snatched from the CIA's files. But it's just a list of running and passing plays."*
> —JOHN MADDEN, *One Knee Equals Two Feet* (1986)

game plan

A specific scheme or plan for achieving some goal. The term comes from football, where it means the specific strategy and tactics, both offensive and defensive, that are devised for a particular game or opponent. The term began to be transferred to business, politics, or any course of action about the middle of the 20th century. Thus an item about Bill Clinton's campaign to win the Democratic nomination had it, "As game-planned with aides last week, Clinton will continue to deny Flowers' specific charges" (*Time*, Feb. 3, 1992).

gamesmanship

The use of tactics to make one's opponent become confused, anxious, and shaky. This term, probably derived from SPORTS-MANSHIP, was invented by British humorist Stephen Potter in his 1947 book, *The Theory and Practice of Gamesmanship, or The Art of Winning Games without Actually Cheating*. It not only entered the language but later gave birth to such related terms as *brinkmanship,* and was quickly extended to describe manipulative machinations that are not strictly illegal but certainly ethically dubious.

game, set, and match
A complete, decisive victory. After the last, deciding game of a tennis match, the umpire traditionally says, "Game, set, and match to Jane Doe." By the second half of the 20th century that term was being transferred to other kinds of winner, as in, "It was game, set, and match to the underwriters of that bond."

Garrison finish
A last-minute surge to victory, in which the winner suddenly comes from behind. The term comes from horse racing and originally alluded to a 19th-century jockey, Edward ("Snapper") Garrison, who was famous for winning races by coming from behind in the homestretch.

> "I'm sick of Slinker's parties . . . let's go and gate-crash something really virtuous."
> —DOROTHY SAYERS, *Murder Must Advertise* (1933)

gate-crasher
A person who attends a performance or social function without a ticket or invitation; an uninvited guest. The term originated in American sports in the early 20th century and began to be transferred to other events by the 1920's, when "crashing" parties became a popular fad among the so-called "smart set."

get a rise out of someone, to
To provoke a strong reaction, usually by teasing or otherwise deliberately irritating a person. The term comes from fishing, where an angler drops a fly in a likely spot and hopes a fish will rise to the floating bait.

get in a huddle: *see* HUDDLE.

get/set/start the ball rolling, to
To get something (a conversation, an undertaking) started. This term presumably originated in bowling or some other game that involves rolling a ball, and began to be used figuratively in the 19th century. "Virginia will keep her ball rolling" appeared in *Log Cabin and Hard Cider Melodies* (1840; cited by *OED*). In cricket the term means to bat first, or take the first knock.

get the hook, to
To be retired. The term is used in baseball for a pitcher who is pulled out of a game, usually because he has given up too many hits. It probably was ultimately derived from fishing.

get to first base: *see* FIRST BASE.

give a body blow: *see* BODY BLOW.

give someone a leg up: *see* LEG UP.

> *"Libertie looses the reynes, and gives you head."*
> —STEPHEN GOSSON, *The Schoole of Abuse* (1579)

give someone his/her head, to
To let a person have his/her own way. This term comes from horsemanship, where it means easing up on the reins and allowing the horse to run freely. It was transferred to human affairs by the 16th century and is still current.

glass jaw
A sensitive person; someone who is easily hurt. The term comes from boxing, where an easily injured fighter is said to have a glass jaw. In baseball the term *glass arm* is used for a pitcher who has a weak arm.

go all the way: *see* ALL THE WAY; GO THE DISTANCE.

go for it

Pursue a goal or activity, regardless of risk. The Americanism *to go for*, dating from the early 19th century, was used with two almost opposite meanings: to be in favor of ("I go for this bill") and to attack ("He was told to go for the robber and get the money back"). The current expression, however, comes from sports, especially football, where coaches exhort players to go for it—that is, to gamble and try to make the necessary yards for a first down instead of kicking to the opposing team on fourth down. It is a risky play, since if it fails the opponents take possession of the ball in a field position usually better than they would have if the ball had been kicked. However, long-time Raider coach John Madden told of a 1976 Pro Bowl game at the Louisiana Superdome, where the gondola is 90 feet above the field. His best punter, Ray Guy, who loved to punt high, asked Madden if it was all right to try to hit it. At first Madden refused but then reconsidered and, since it was an all-star game and an exhibition, he told Guy, "On second thought, go for it." Guy actually managed to hit the gondola, but the officials decided that the play was illegal and the ball would have to be re-punted, and it was.

In baseball, when a batter is told to *go for the fences*, he is being told to try for a home run. In Olympic competition, contenders are told to *go for the gold*, meaning to go for the top medal; indeed, this was the quasi-official slogan of the Olympic Games of 1980.

golf ball

A ball-shaped printing element used in some electric typewriters. Its name, of course, comes from the fact that it resembles the ball used in golf. Although the name "golf ball" has been around since the 16th century, the kind of ball used in the game has changed over the centuries. Early golf balls included one called a "feathery," a leather casing stuffed with feathers, and a "gutty," made of the brownish-red gum substance called gutta-percha. The latter, it was found, had a much truer trajectory after it had been used for a time and became damaged. Consequently manufacturers began to apply "damage marks" to new balls, and this "dimple" ball is universally used today. The typewriter element resembles it in that all the elements of type are mounted on the ball, giving it the same dimpled appearance. It was first made by IBM in the 1960's but has, like the electric typewriter itself, been largely replaced by word processors.

> "We had two swift and pleasant hours—and then . . .
> into the hangar, where the white golf cart waited for
> us."
>
> —LADY BIRD JOHNSON, White House Diary (1964)

golf cart
A battery-powered cart used to transport a small number of persons over a relatively short distance. It was developed about 1950 to transport golfers and their equipment around the course. It soon was found useful for other purposes, such as moving travelers and their luggage between gates in an airport, transporting elderly alumni around the campus during a class reunion, or taking guests from their rooms to the pool or tennis court in a spacious resort. See also CADDIE CART.

> "Eric: My wife says if I don't give
> up golf she'll leave me.
> Ernie: That's terrible.
> Eric: I know—I'm really going to
> miss her."
>
> —ERIC MORECAMBE and ERNIE WISE,
> The Morecambe and Wise Joke Book (1979)

golf widow
A woman whose husband is so occupied with a sport or hobby of some kind that the couple spend almost no leisure time together. The term, of course, originally alluded to the woman

abandoned in favor of the golf course and still has this meaning. One writer suggests that some golf widows get revenge
by taking a very non-athletic lover. The term, which dates
from about 1890, later was extended to other sports and activities, sometimes unchanged even though golf was not involved. However, the *Boston Globe* obituary for Elizabeth
Lapchick, who had been married to the famous basketball
player and coach Joe Lapchick for forty-one years, said she
became famous for being the first *basketball widow*.

good innings

A long turn at something—running a business, remaining in
public office, or simply living a long time. The term comes
from cricket, where an innings is that part of the game played
by either side while at bat, and a "good innings" means that
the side has scored many runs. It was transferred in the 19th
century but is heard more often in Britain than America.
However, Katherine Hall Page has it in *The Body in the
Bouillon* (1991), a murder mystery set in New England: "I
heard about the soup mishap. I hope you're not feeling upset
about it. Farley [the murder victim] had some good innings."

> "*Show me a good and gracious loser and I'll show you
> a failure.*"
> —Attributed to football coach KNUTE ROCKNE, 1920's

good loser/sport

An individual who shows grace in defeat. Both of these terms
have been around for at least a century and have long been
transferred from athletic contests to any other kind of competition, as well as to noncompetitive forms of adversity. However, as the quotation above suggests, some athletes regard
such behavior as a defeatist attitude that will inevitably hurt
one's future performance. In keeping with this idea, Hall of
Famer Ernie Banks, rationalizing about the less than ideal
record of the Chicago Cubs one season, was quoted as saying,
"The only way to prove you're a good sport is to lose." But

H. A. Harris, in his history of British sport, wrote, "Today it is unfashionable to say so, but it nevertheless remains true that the greatest gift of those Victorian pioneers to sport was their insistence on the importance of being a good loser" (*Sport in Britain*, 1975). See also POOR SPORT/SORE LOSER; SPORTSMANSHIP.

go the distance, to
To complete something. The term originated in boxing, where it is used in two ways, to last for all of the rounds that have been scheduled, or to last for all of the rounds without a knockout or technical knockout. The latter (lasting without a knockout) also is put as to *go all the way*. In baseball "going the distance" means to pitch an entire game. Another variant is to *go the route*. See also ALL THE WAY.

go to bat for (someone/something), to
To take someone's side; to support an idea or defend a cause, etc. The term comes from baseball, where it simply designates a substitute batter, but it is the notion of supporting one's team in this way that has been transferred to more general use. Thus, one might say, "A good friend will go to bat for her, even if he thinks she has no chance of getting the job."

> " 'There'll be time enough for that later,' Baker said. . . . Some things aren't worth going to the mat for, and this was one of them."
> —J. A. JANCE, *Payment in Kind* (1991)

go to the mat, to
To fight in a determined way. The term comes from wrestling, where it signifies hanging onto one's opponent even when both are down (the mat being the padded floor covering used in bouts). It was transferred to mean other kinds of struggle by the early 20th century.

*"Four Champions Face Off for $1,000,000! PGA Grand
Slam, Live Today, Tomorrow."*
—Newspaper ad for TV program, 1991

grand slam

A total victory or sweeping success. Although this term originated in whist and related card games (notably bridge),
where it means the winning of all thirteen tricks by one side,
it is also used in baseball, tennis, and golf. In baseball it denotes a home run hit with (all three) bases loaded, resulting in
four runs for the team. More than a century ago, in 1890, Sil-
ver Bill Phillips of the Pittsburgh Pirates became the only (so
far) major-league pitcher to allow two grand slams in a single
inning. On just two bad pitches, he allowed the Chicago Cubs
to score eight runs.

In tennis a grand slam means winning all four national
championships—the Australian Open, French Open, Wimbledon, and United States Open—in a single calendar year, a feat
achieved to date (in singles play) only by Don Budge (1938),
Maureen Connolly (1953), Rod Laver (twice, 1962, 1969), Mar-
garet Smith Court (1970), and Steffi Graf (1988). In golf it
similarly means winning all four major championships—the
British Open, U.S. Open, Professional Golfer's Association,
and Masters Golf Tournament. The term is also transferred to
similar victories in an entire series of contests, or to any com-
prehensive success.

"To faint or fall over would be a grand-stand play."
—M. D. POST, *Harvard Stories* (1893)

grandstand play, to make a

To show off. This term, which alludes to the section of permanent stands used to accommodate spectators at ballparks,
race courses, and similar outdoor athletic sites, was first used
in the 19th century for the antics of baseball players and
other athletes. Specifically, it means making a spectacular
play that is calculated to please the crowd more than to be

strategically effective. A player known to engage in this behavior is called a *grandstander*. Also see HOT-DOG.

ground rules
Basic rules or procedures of conduct. The term comes from
baseball, where it refers to specific regulations for a particular ballpark, based on abnormal conditions such as unusu-
ally high or close outfield fences, or a field obstruction of
some kind. The most common kind of ground rule specifies
that a ball is dead and therefore the runner may advance a
certain number of bases. For example, in Detroit's Tiger
Stadium, a batted ball that hits the flag pole in deep center
field above a yellow stripe about nine feet off the ground
and then bounces into the stands is automatically ruled a
home run.

Other ground rules do not necessarily allude to the
unique conditions in a park but award two or three bases to
the batter and all runners in special situations. Among the
best-known is the *ground-rule double*, a two-base hit given a
batter and advancing all base runners two bases when the ball
lands in fair territory but bounces over an outfield wall or into
the stands. Even though a runner on first base might score if
the ball did not bounce out of reach, under the rule the runner
must stop at third base. A similar rule allows everyone to advance two bases if a fair ball goes through the outfield fence,
through or under a scoreboard, or through or under shrubs or
vines on a fence, or if it gets stuck in a fence, scoreboard,
shrubs, or vines. In all these cases the ball is considered
dead. However, there are still other so-called ground rules
where the ball remains in play and the batter or runners
can try to advance farther than the automatic two or three
bases, at their own risk. These are: two bases automatically
if a fielder deliberately throws his glove at a thrown ball
and the glove touches the ball; three bases if a fielder
throws his glove at a fair batted ball and the glove touches it;
two bases if a fielder deliberately touches a thrown ball
with his cap, mask, or any other detached part of his uniform;
and three bases if a fielder deliberately touches a fair batted

ball with his cap, mask, or any other detached part of his uniform.

Baseball's ground rules date from the 1880's. The term was transferred to other events about the mid-20th century, in such locutions as "The ground rules for this press conference exclude questions about the candidate's personal life."

hail Mary play

A maneuver attempted against heavy odds, often in a time of desperation. The term comes from football, where it means a last-ditch attempt to score because time is running out. Such maneuvers include throwing to a receiver who is not clearly open, throwing into a crowd, or throwing an extremely long pass. Its name, from the familiar prayer beginning with the words "Hail Mary," alludes to the fact that the passer is, in effect, praying that the throw will succeed.

A famous example occurred in 1984, when Boston College quarterback Doug Flutie threw a long pass into Miami's end zone. It was caught by his roommate, Gerard Phelan, for a touchdown that put Boston into the 1985 Cotton Bowl against Houston (which they won, 45–28). The term was transferred to other long-shot maneuvers in the second half of the 20th century. For example, in the Persian Gulf War of 1991 Allied troops were lined up on Saudi soil, and between them and Kuwait City stood the entire Iraqi force. A French battalion, making a wide arc around both lines, moved some 150 miles behind the Iraqis and mounted a successful attack, which in effect ended the war. In the press conference that followed, Allied commander General Schwartzkopf called the maneuver a hail Mary play.

halftime

A period signifying the midpoint of any activity. Although in Britain it was used from the early 19th century for the midpoint of the school year, in America the term originally was used mainly for the midpoint of a football game, as it still is. In both college and professional football, it signifies a fifteen-minute rest period between the second and third quarters of the game (as opposed to one-minute rest periods between the first and second quarters, and the third and fourth quarters). The teams retire to their locker rooms, and the spectators usually are treated to a more or less elaborate show with marching bands, baton twirlers, and the like. In the locker room, long-time coach John Madden maintains, "What goes on at halftime isn't what most people think.... There's no time for a fiery talk, not if you want to use your time the way you should use it: to prepare your team mentally for the second half" (*One Knee Equals Two Feet*, 1986).

Basketball games also have a halftime, in college basketball, between the two 20-minute halves, and in professional basketball, between the second and third of the 15-minute quarters.

Hall of Fame
A number of individuals who have been selected as outstanding in their particular field. Although the first Hall of Fame, established in New York City around the turn of the century, honored outstanding Americans in a variety of fields (politics, the arts, etc.), the term today is more closely attached to those Halls of Fame that honor great athletes. (Moreover, the related noun *Hall of Famer* always refers to athletes.) The first of these was the Baseball Hall of Fame, established at Cooperstown, New York, in 1939, the centennial year of baseball. It was followed by some twenty-two others, among them the Professional Football Hall of Fame, Basketball Hall of Fame, and Automobile Racing Hall of Fame. "If you hang around long enough you'll end up somewhere," said football great Johnny Unitas when he was elected to the Football Hall of Fame (Jan. 29, 1979).

handicap
A disadvantage or disability; also, a compensation for such a disadvantage. This word is thought to have originated as *hand in cap*, an ancient game (called Newe Faire in 14th-century Britain) in which two players put the same amount of money in an umpire's cap, and also offered each other some article in trade. The umpire decided how much more money was needed to make the inferior of the two articles the same value as the other. If the players disagreed with the umpire's judgment, each kept his own item and the umpire kept the

money in the cap. If they agreed with the umpire, they traded the two articles and the umpire got the forfeit money. If only one player agreed, there was no exchange and that player kept the forfeit money.

In the late 17th century elements of this game, including the name, were transferred to horse racing. At first entrants drew lots from the umpire's cap to decide which horse would run closest to the rail (the best position), and the umpire also would assess the different weights of the horses and allocate the weights they would carry so as to give each horse an equal chance to win. Thus a weak horse would be assigned less weight, and a strong horse more. *Handicap* then came to mean any contest in which the superior competitor was given a disadvantage, and in time the disadvantage itself was called "handicap." By the 1860's it was used for any kind of disadvantage, and by 1900 or so it was being applied to a physical or mental disability in an individual.

In other sports as well, a handicap denotes an advantage given to the weak or a disadvantage imposed on the strong. Handicaps take numerous forms, but most often they consist of adding or deducting points from a competitor's score, or conferring a time, distance, or weight advantage in a race. In bowling, a handicap is an agreed-on number of points added to an individual or team score so as to permit balanced competition. In golf it is a specific number of strokes an amateur may subtract from the score so as to compete fairly with better players. (A golfer's handicap is based on the number of strokes he regularly plays over the course handicap rating and is calculated as 85 percent of the average difference between the rating and the player's ten lowest rounds in the last twenty rounds.) In sailing when boats of different type or size are competing, an individual allowance based on length, width, sail area, past performance, and similar factors is subtracted from each entrant's elapsed time. When automobiles of different classes race against one another, the weaker may be given the starting signal before the stronger, whereas in track a weaker runner may start a given distance in front of the others.

The verb form, *to handicap*, means to try predicting the

winner of a contest of any kind by comparing the past performance of the competitors or to assigning odds for (or
against) the competitors. In general usage the verb, too, was
transferred so as to mean placing someone at a disadvantage
(as in "The alkaline soil in his garden really handicaps his attempts to grow acid-loving shrubs").

*"The most despised, scorned, and spat-upon person in
politics today is the handler."*
                    —WILLIAM SAFIRE, *New York Times,* Nov. 24, 1991

handler
A coach who helps orchestrate the image of a public figure.
The term originated in dog shows, where it was used for the
owner or trainer charged with showing off the points of a dog
at a trial. By the mid-20th century it was adopted in boxing,
to designate the chief second or assistant second who stands
in the boxer's corner between rounds to encourage and advise
him. Jack Dempsey used it in a 1950 book: "His handlers
threw in the towel"—that is, asked the referee to stop the
fight (cited by William Safire in the article quoted above).
Great boxers generally have equally great handlers: Chappie
Blackburn for Joe Louis; Angelo Dundee for Sugar Ray Leonard and Muhammad Ali; Cus D'Amato for Floyd Patterson
and Mike Tyson. The term was transferred to politics in the
1980's and became particularly prominent in the 1988 presidential campaign of George Bush, who not only had superb
handlers but, after becoming president himself, lent their assistance to other Republican candidates. Some consider "handler" a pejorative term, with its implications of manipulating
a political candidate like a prizefighter, or worse yet, a dog.
The handlers themselves prefer such names as "media consultant" or "policy adviser," while those they handle tend to refer to them as "aides" or "staff members."

hand-off

The transference of control of an aircraft from one control center to another. This term came from American football, where a hand-off is the transference of the ball from one player (usually the quarterback) to a teammate. (In rugby it has a different meaning, the action of pushing off an opponent.) The football term dates from about 1940. It gave rise to the aviation term in the 1970's.

hands down

Easily and with certainty. This expression comes from horse racing, where a jockey drops his or her hands and relaxes hold on the reins when winning the race is a certainty; he or she is then said to *win hands down*. By the mid-19th century this term was transferred to other enterprises, as in "Her performance was sure to win an Oscar, hands down."

handsprings, to do

To negotiate something with ease. Literally handsprings are a gymnastic feat in which only the feet and hands touch the floor, and the gymnast, on passing through a momentary handstand, pushes up with the arms to complete a somersault. It differs from cartwheels in that the performer moves either forward or backward rather than sideways. This 19th-century term was transferred to other undertakings about the mid-20th century, as in "She's a much better speaker than her husband; she can do handsprings around him."

hang up the gloves, to

To retire. The ultimate origin of this expression, which in its current form alludes to the retirement of a boxer, probably is giving up one's weapon; the earliest citation in *OED* dates from the 13th century and quotes Robert of Gloucester hanging up his ax. In similar fashion, later writers speak of giving up a sword or gun. Boxing gloves became standard equipment only in the latter part of the 19th century, whence this expression dates. It began to be used figuratively for other kinds of retirement in the 20th century.

hardball: *see* PLAY HARDBALL.

hat trick

Three successive identical achievements by the same person; an extraordinary feat. The term originated in cricket, where, in the 1880's, it was customary to give the prize of a new hat to a bowler who took three wickets with three consecutively bowled balls. The term was extended with a similar meaning (but no hat award) to numerous other sports: ice hockey and soccer, where it means three goals scored by a single player in the same game; horse racing, three wins in three consecutive races by a jockey, or winning the same annual race in three successive years; and, but only very rarely, in baseball, one player hitting a single, double, triple, and home run (in any order) in one game (this feat is more often called *hitting for the cycle*). Still later it was transferred to a similar achievement in any area—such as a lawyer winning three successive cases—as well as being used more loosely for an especially adroit maneuver. There is at least one instance of its application to football, cited by the late John Ciardi. In the 1981 Super Bowl game, Oakland Raider Rod Martin intercepted three Philadelphia Eagle passes, and a sportscaster described his feat as a hat trick.

have one's innings, to

To have an opportunity; to take one's turn. This expression comes from cricket, where it signifies having one's turn at bat.

It is more widely used in Britain than in America. Also see
GOOD INNINGS.

have something on the ball: *see* ON THE BALL.

haymaker
A devastating blow. This term comes from boxing slang,
which took it from its original sense of tossing and spreading
hay. In prizefighting a haymaker is a powerful punch, usually
one that knocks out the opponent ("flattening" him probably
is the analogy to spreading hay). It dates from the early 20th
century, and by the 1930's was being used figuratively for any
powerful blow. Also see SUNDAY PUNCH.

   *"You and Peaches . . . had a superficial head-start
   with prettiness."*
                          —F. SCOTT FITZGERALD, letter, 1935

head start
An early start or some other special advantage in a competition. The term dates from late 19th-century racing, when a
horse might be given an advantage of several lengths over the
others. It was being used figuratively by the early 20th century. In the 1960's the U.S. government began to sponsor a
program of preschool education for disadvantaged youngsters
called *Head Start*.

heads up
Watch out; pay attention. This interjection, now used in numerous situations where the speaker is calling for alertness, is
always stated in the plural, whether it is addressed to one
person or several. It originated in sports and is most often
shouted out to baseball spectators to keep them from getting
beaned by a foul ball. In other sports it may be uttered by a
coach exhorting his or her charges to be alert for a particular
move by the opponent(s). It also is heard on the tennis court,
when a player is alerting his or her doubles partner that the

opponent may be preparing for a smash or hitting down the alley or some similar maneuver.

hear footsteps, to
To be distracted from one's course by fear of imminent danger. The term comes from football, where it refers to a player being distracted by fear of being imminently hit or tackled by an approaching opponent. It often leads to an error in play, such as a hurried throw by the quarterback or a dropped catch by a receiver.

> "*In 1960, almost all the heavy hitters ran—Johnson, Symington, Humphrey, along with a much less senior figure named John F. Kennedy.*"
> —R. W. APPLE, JR., *New York Times,* Feb. 16, 1992

heavy hitter
A powerful person, who is very important and/or influential. The term probably originated in boxing, where it refers to a fighter who relies on powerful slugging rather than skill or dexterity. In football it refers to a player with the reputation of being a punishing blocker or tackler. John Madden, writing about Jack Tatum, said his high school coaches told him to hit hard, and ... "he was All-American because he hit hard. In the NFL, he was on three Pro Bowl teams because he hit hard" (*Hey, Wait a Minute,* 1984). Finally, in baseball a batter who is often successful is sometimes called a heavy hitter, although he is more often called a POWER HITTER. The term was transferred to politics (as in the quotation above, from an article bearing the headline "Democrats Dread a Season Without Heavy Hitters") and other arenas in the second half of the 20th century. Thus *Publishers Weekly* had it "The heaviest hitters in the magazine industry are reputedly losing their collective grip" (Aug. 10, 1990).

"Is Mendelssohn a Heavyweight? Festival Puts Him on the Scales."
—Headline, *New York Times*, Aug. 20, 1991

heavyweight
Especially important or meaningful. This 19th-century term, originally simply describing considerable poundage, quickly became a particular weight division in boxing, today established at more than 175 pounds (179–200 pounds for amateurs). It also is used in weightlifting, for a weight of 110 kilograms (242.5 pounds), and wrestling, for a weight up to 100 kilograms (220.4 pounds). By about 1900 it was being used figuratively for anything or anyone of imposing importance.

"He shoots—he scores!"
He succeeds! This expression, always uttered with enthusiasm and, sometimes, surprise, comes from ice hockey. According to Stu Hackel of the National Hockey League, it was coined by the Canadian broadcaster Foster Hewitt, who pioneered play-by-play radio broadcasts of this sport in 1923 (as reported by William Safire of the *New York Times*). Scoring in hockey is relatively infrequent relative to attempts to score, hence the enthusiasm and surprise in this exclamation.

hidden ball trick
A deceptive maneuver. This term comes from baseball, where it describes several moves, both legal and illegal. The definitely illegal one involves bringing a second ball into play. It also refers to a baseman concealing the ball so that he can tag out a runner, as well as to a pitcher's ability to hide the ball from the batter's view until delivering it (so as to conceal his grip, and therefore the kind of pitch).

In 1916 New York Giants second baseman Larry Doyle used the hidden ball trick to tag out Rabbit Maranville of the Boston Braves, where upon his teammates kidded him unmercifully about falling for this sucker play. Moreover, at dinner that evening at their hotel, the chef brought out a special dessert for him—a plate of ice cream topped with cherries and whipped cream—and when Rabbit began to eat it, he found a baseball hidden inside.

high dive, to take a

To take a risky position. The transfer from literal to figurative took place in the mid-20th century. The high board in diving competitions is three meters (9.8 feet) above the water, and executing a perfect dive from this height takes considerable skill. The expression has been transferred to other risky maneuvers, as in "He's taking a high dive in the market with all these short-sale transactions."

high five

A congratulatory gesture in which one slaps one's raised palm and fingers against those of another. The practice originated in one or another team sport in which teammates celebrated a winning move or game in this way. The University of Louisville basketball team claimed to have been the first to start the practice in 1979, but this origin is by no means certain. In any event, the gesture soon became common practice off athletic fields and now is sometimes used simply as one of goodwill toward one's colleagues or friends.

high-sticking
Underhanded behavior. This mid-20th century term comes
from ice hockey, where it designates holding the stick with
the blade above shoulder level (more than four feet high in
amateur play) so as to hit an opponent, which usually invokes
a penalty. It was later transferred to other kinds of nastiness.

hike: *see* TAKE A HIKE.

> *"To me the ultimate human experience is to witness
> the flawless execution of the hit and run."*
> —Attributed to baseball general manager BRANCH RICKEY

hit-and-run
Fleeing the scene of an accident, particularly one involving a
vehicle, that one has caused. The term originated around the
turn of the century in baseball, where it refers to a play in
which the runner on first base breaks for second base on the
pitch, and the batter hits into an area left unguarded by the
infield (which has moved to cover second base to prevent a
steal). Normally with a left-handed batter the shortstop
moves to second base, while with a right-handed batter the
second baseman covers second, but this procedure varies
depending on the precise circumstances.

Allegedly the hit-and-run play was created by the Baltimore Orioles in the 1890's. The term was transferred to automobile collisions in which the driver fled the scene of the
accident in the 1930's. By the 1960's it was further extended
to any situation where a concentrated attack was followed by
rapid flight, particularly military maneuvers of this nature
("hit-and-run raids").

hit or miss
Haphazard, at random. This term presumably comes from
archery, or at least from target practice, and has been used
figuratively since the 16th century, when it was sometimes
put as *hittie missie* (as by Thomas Wilson in *The Art of*

Rhetorique, 1553). Randle Cotgrave even defined it in his 1611 dictionary, "hittie missie; here or there, one way or other."

hit the mark
To the point; to be right. Originating in archery, the term alludes to hitting the target, an accurate shot being described as a good *marksman*. The term has been used figuratively since at least the 16th century. Samuel Butler had it in *Hudibras* (1663), "The fairest mark is easiest hit." For the opposite, see MISS THE MARK.

hold with the hare and run with the hounds, to
To stick up for both sides in a conflict; to be two-faced. The term comes from hunting, where, of course, it is impossible to side with both the quarry and the hunter. The term was already being used proverbially in the 15th century, when an anonymous writer had it: "Thou hast a crokyd tunge heldyng with hownd and wyth hare."

hole-in-one
A perfect achievement. The term comes from golf, where it denotes a perfect stroke, that is, driving the ball from the tee into a hole with a single stroke. The longest such shot ever made was 447 yards by Bob Mitera into the tenth hole at Miracle Hill, Omaha, Nebraska, in 1965. The first woman to score two holes-in-one in a single round was Mrs. W. Driver at Balgowlah Club, in New South Wales, Australia, in 1942. Consecutive holes-in-one are even rarer.

> "Home-run hitters: Scientific serials literature (which is purported to have doubled over the last decade) continues to thrive."
> —*Publishers Weekly*, Aug. 10, 1990

home run
Also, *homer*. A high-scoring achievement; doubling one's profits. This term originated in baseball in the mid-19th century to designate a hit that enables the batter to round all the

bases, reach home plate, and score a run. Most home runs are hit outside the ballpark, but occasionally one is hit inside the park. The first major-league home-run king was the National League's George Hall, who scored five homers for Philadelphia in 1876. That achievement pales beside that of Babe Ruth, long known as "the home-run king" for his 1927 record of 60 homers. Even after the New York Yankees Roger Maris broke that record in 1961 with 61 homers, most people still associate homers with Ruth, who once complained, "If I make a home run every time I bat, they think I'm all right; if I don't, they think they can call me anything they like" (quoted in Robert W. Creamer, *Babe: The Legend Comes to Life*). For career home runs, Ruth's record 714 was beaten by Hank Aaron's 755.

The term "home run" is also loosely used in football and basketball for a spectacular scoring play, such as a long touchdown pass in the former or a three-point field goal in the latter. In Britain "home run" is sometimes used in the same meaning as HOMESTRETCH.

The figurative use of "home run" dates from the second half of the 20th century. In the securities business it means doubling one's money on an investment—for example, buying a stock at 14 and selling it a short time later at 28. In other areas it means a similar gain, as seen in the quotation above. Occasionally the achievement is put slightly differently. A *Wall Street Journal* headline had it: "Nintendo Boss Rounds Third in Mariners Bid" (June 10, 1992), for a story concerning the virtual certainty that Nintendo Co. would acquire the Seattle Mariners baseball team. To *round third* means, of course, being on the way to success, that is, scoring a run.

Hitting home runs is, needless to say, very satisfying for a batter, while giving them up is exactly the opposite for a pitcher. However, Oakland A's pitcher Catfish Hunter made light of it after he gave up two homers to the Los Angeles Dodgers in the 1974 World Series: "I had some friends here from North Carolina and they'd never seen a home run, so I gave them a couple."

"Already we see the slave States of Maryland and Missouri, Arkansas and Louisiana, and others, on the home-stretch to become free."
— REP. HULBURD of New York, House of
Representatives speech, Mar. 12, 1864

homestretch
The final phase of any undertaking. The term comes from horse racing, where it signifies the portion of the racetrack between the last turn and the finish line. (In Britain this is called the "home run.") The term has been used figuratively since the mid-19th century.

"Let us root, root, root for the home team,
If they don't win, it's a shame. . . ."
— JACK NORWORTH, *Take Me Out to the Ball Game* (1908)

home team
Colleagues from one's own base of operations. The term comes from baseball and other sports where teams travel about to compete in their opponents' stadiums and ballparks as well as their own. When playing at their own base, they are the home team and usually attract a large crowd of cheering fans. When playing at their opponents' base, they can expect much less spectator support. In the late 20th century the term has occasionally been used figuratively, as in a multinational organization for the personnel of a domestic division.

hook, line, and sinker
Completely. This 19-century Americanism comes from fishing and alludes to a fish taking in bait so completely that it swallows not only the baited hook but also the line and sinker. It has been used figuratively since at least 1900. Mystery writer Zelda Popkin had it in her *No Crime for a Lady* (1942): "Innocent enough to swallow it, hook, line, and sinker."

"Gamesters and race-horses never last long."
— GEORGE HERBERT, *Jacula Prudentum* (1640)

horse player

A habitual gambler. Horse racing has been a venue for betting practically since its beginnings, and in the late 18th century betting on horses began to be formalized (see under BOOKIE). *Playing the horses* (i.e., betting on races) came into the language in the 1940's, whence the term "horse player" for one who does so. In succeeding decades the term was used figuratively for any habitual bettor and, by extension, risk-taker.

"It is difference of opinion that makes horse races."
— MARK TWAIN, *Pudd'nhead Wilson* (1893)

horse race

A formidable contest, whose outcome is difficult to predict. The figurative use of this expression, which is current mainly in America, dates from the second half of the 20th century. It has been applied especially to politics, as, for example, "This year's primary is really a horse race among three candidates."

horses

Power. Some consider this term an abbreviation of horsepower, which would preclude its place in this book, and indeed it has been so used colloquially in Britain since about 1900. However, in America it also has long been associated with team sports such as baseball, where it refers to the players who are responsible for the team's offense, as in "The best coach won't help the team win if he doesn't have the horses." By the mid-20th century it was transferred to other undertakings, as, for example, "A small company like ours just doesn't have the horses to compete against a giant like General Electric."

hot-dog, to

To show off. Many authorities believe the frankfurter-bun combination we call "hot dog" originated in a ballpark (via vendor Harry Mozley Stevens at the New York Giants' stadium, the Polo Grounds, in the early 1900's). The noun, which also became an expression of delight or excellence (as in "Hot dog!"), then was turned into a verb, probably also at a ball-park, though it is no longer clear exactly where or when. At first it referred to showy, intricate maneuvers. Soon, however, it acquired the connotation of showing off, and then it was transferred to other sports, notably surfing and skiing. Still mainly American slang, the expression has come into general use for any kind of bravura display.

> *"Act while thy hand is hot."*
> —SENECA, *Hercules Oetaeus,* C. A.D. 60

hot hand
A temporary ability to do extremely well at something. The term comes from basketball, where it is used for a player who, during a particular stretch in a game, is very adept at making baskets and seemingly never misses. Fascinated by this no-tion, Princeton economist Burton Malkiel made a statistical study that in the end proved this theory to be a myth. A 1980's study of the Philadelphia 76ers over one and one-half seasons showed that a hit followed by a miss is more likely than making two baskets in a row. The outcomes of previous shots, Malkiel concluded, influenced the players' predictions but not their performance. Nevertheless, the idea is believed widely enough so that the term came to be used figuratively for anyone with temporarily heightened ability, as in "My bro-ker's got the hot hand at picking stocks today."

> *"For when the one Great Scorer comes*
> *To write against your name,*
> *He marks, not that you won or lost—*
> *But how you played the game."*
> —GRANTLAND RICE, *Alumnus Football* (1927)

how you play the game
An honorable process is more important than a successful out-come. The thought was already expressed in the 5th century

B.C. by the Greek historian Herodotus. Writing about the Olympic Games, where the prize was simply a crown of olives, he wrote, " 'Tis not for money they contend but for glory" (*History*, c. 445 B.C.). The current locution, often preceded by "it's not whether you win or lose," comes from the most famous lines ever penned by sports journalist and poet Grantland Rice (1854–1954), quoted above. It is heard not only on playing fields but has been transferred to other endeavors, albeit sometimes ruefully, after sustaining a loss.

"*It* [football] *is committee meetings called huddles, separated by outbursts of violence.*"
—GEORGE F. WILL, *Newsweek*, Sept. 6, 1976

huddle
A more or less secret meeting to discuss a plan of action. The term with this specific meaning comes from the football field, where a huddle (brief meeting) of the offensive team is held between downs, usually in a circle behind the line of scrimmage, where the quarterback issues instructions and signals (see CALL THE SIGNALS). The offense then proceeds with play as directed in the huddle.

Although the noun "huddle" had meant a mass of things crowded together since the 16th century, the connotation of this meaning was confusion and disorder. The current locution, with its idea of strategic planning, comes from football and has been extended to practically any circumstances. Thus Joyce Wadler, writing about her breast surgery, has it, "When ... I tell them I would feel very silly being pushed down the hall on a bed, they [the nurses] go into a huddle, bend the rules, and alert pre-op on a walkie-talkie" (*New York* magazine, Apr. 20, 1992).

Of course, both on the football field and elsewhere, the best-laid plans made in a huddle can go amiss. Players sometimes forget what has been decided in the huddle. John Madden writes of a Super Bowl game in which Dolphin quarterback Bob Griese forgot what he had said in a first-quarter huddle on the Vikings' five-yard line. In this case, Madden reports, Griese had to call new signals, and in the end the Viking defense was as confused as the Dolphin offense (*One Knee Equals Two Feet*, 1986).

hurdle, to

To overcome (difficulties, a problem, etc.). The term comes from various sports that involve leaping over obstacles. Among these are track events called *hurdles*, in which runners must leap over barriers placed at intervals on the track, and *hurdle racing*, or *steeplechasing*, in which riders must urge their mounts to jump over obstacles (walls, fences, etc.). The latter was invented by the Prince Regent of England, and the first such race, which involved jumping in and over sheep pens, took place in Bristol in 1821. The track event also originated in England, the first hurdles competition being held at Oxford University in 1864, where runners had to jump over sheep fences. In one sport, football, hurdling is illegal. A ball-carrier jumping feet first over an opponent still on his feet invokes a fifteen-yard penalty for his team.

The ultimate origin of hurdling was in warfare, where defenders set up barriers against attackers, and indeed the word *hurdle* itself dates from the 13th century. The transfer to sporting events took place in the 19th century, and to other kinds of obstacle by the 20th century.

I call 'em as I see 'em: *see* CALL 'EM.

"I'm the greatest"
An assertion of one's excellence, often spoken ironically. It is a direct quotation of boxer Muhammad Ali (originally named Cassius Clay), who in the 1960's became known for his fast talking and outrageous boasting. After he won the Olympic gold medal, he said, "I'm not the greatest; I'm the double greatest. Not only do I knock 'em out, I pick the round" (*New York Times*, Dec. 9, 1962).

> "*A skilful huntsman . . . who generally contrived to be in at the death.*"
> —EDWARD BULWER-LYTTON, *Night and Morning* (1841)

in at the death/finish
Present at the literal or figurative demise of something or someone—the collapse of an organization, the failure of a plan, etc. The term comes from fox hunting, where it literally designated the hunters' presence at the death of a fox they had run to ground. It was already being used figuratively in other situations by about 1800.

infighting
A struggle among the members of a group. The term comes from prizefighting, where since about 1800 it has denoted a boxer fighting very close to his opponent, as in a clinch (see also CLINCH). It was transferred to in-house contention of various kinds about the middle of the 20th century. A closely related word is *infighter*, which in fencing as well as in boxing refers to a person who fights at close quarters. Figuratively, it has been used for a tough, ruthless opponent of any kind since about 1970.

*"Will you . . . run upon a Christenbody, with full cry and
open mouth?"*

—RICHARD HARVEY, *Plaine Percevall
the Peace-maker of England* (1589)

in full cry
In hot pursuit. This term comes from the sport of hunting,
where the word "cry" has meant the yelping of hounds in a
chase since the early 16th century. It soon was being used figuratively as well, in such turns of phrase as "A pack of journalists were behind the minister in full cry."

inning, innings
An opportunity to perform; a turn. In America an *inning* is a
turn or period of play in numerous sports—baseball, badminton, billiards, bowling, croquet, curling, handball, horseshoes,
and trapshooting, to name the most important of them. In
cricket an *innings* is a turn at bat for either an individual
batsman or a team (side). The American version is occasionally used figuratively simply to mean having a turn at anything. The British one has given rise to numerous metaphors
used on both sides of the Atlantic: see EARLY INNINGS; GOOD
INNINGS; HAVE ONE'S INNINGS.

in play
Under attack. The term comes from numerous sports—
football, soccer, hockey—in which a ball or puck is said to be
in play during an ongoing offense. In the late 20th century the
term began to be used as business slang. Thus a corporation
that raiders or investors were attempting to take over was
said to be in play, even if it succeeded in fighting off the attack.

inside game, the
The use of skillful tactics, relying on details known only to
true aficionados. This term originated about 1900 as *inside
ball* or *inside baseball*, where it denoted a game played with
careful attention to the finer points of the sport and good

teamwork, as opposed to reliance on sheer power. New York Giants pitcher Christy Mathewson (who won twenty or more games every year for thirteen years, made a total of 2,499 strikeouts, and won 373 games in his career) had it, "For eight and one-third innings the Giants had played 'inside' ball, and I had carefully nursed along every batter who came to the plate, studying his weakness and pitching at it" (*Pitching*, 1912). It has occasionally been used figuratively for similar tactics in other activities, but is heard less often nowadays.

> "*It gave him the inside track, as the sporting men say, with reference to any rival.*"
>
> —OLIVER WENDELL HOLMES, *Guardian Angel* (1867)

inside track, the

A position of special advantage. The term comes from horse racing and alludes to the inner, or shorter, track of the course, on which it is easier to win. Originating in the 19th century, the term was being used figuratively for any advantageous position by the mid-19th century. An 1857 edition of a Richmond, Virginia, newspaper had: "In a word, '*Gizzard-Foot*' has the inside track for the Senatorship and means to keep it."

In automobile racing the inside track is called the *pole*, and to be in the *pole position* or *sitting on the pole* carries a similar advantage. In the Indy 500 and other important races drivers compete beforehand in order to qualify for the pole position. At this writing, however, these terms are used figuratively only rarely.

in someone's corner, to be

To be on someone's side. The term refers to the corner of the boxing ring, where a fighter's seconds go to attend him between rounds. Its literal use dates from the mid-19th century. According to the London Prize-Ring Rules of 1853, "The combatants . . . shall retire until the seconds of each have tossed for choice of position, which adjusted, the winner shall choose as his corner and conduct his man thereto." The term began to be used figuratively in the first half of the 20th century, as in "The boss expects his staff to stay in his corner while the new chairman gets settled."

instant replay
A repetition or near duplication of an event. The term comes from sports coverage, where a particular play or shot often is repeated via videotape immediately after its completion. This practice became common in the early 1960's, and the term began to be used figuratively for any kind of repetition a decade or two later.

At first, instant replay was purely for the benefit of the television audience, but for a time it was employed to help officials when they were uncertain about a ruling. However, in 1992 the owners of the National Football League announced they were eliminating instant replay for the purpose of reversing officials' decisions for that season, to the distress of some coaches. Miami Dolphins coach Don Shula held that the previous year had seen 81 reversals in Miami's games, plays that were miscalled on the field but corrected by replay. However, broadcasters can still use the replay, which helps the home audience, who cannot always see exactly what happens the first time around.

interference: *see* RUN INTERFERENCE

in the bag
Certain to succeed. This term comes from hunting and refers to the container in which hunters placed small game, called a "bag" since the 15th century. It began to be used figuratively for a virtual certainty in the 20th century, at first in America. The *Emporia Gazette* used the phrase in describing Gene Tunney's victory over heavyweight champion Jack Dempsey in 1926: "After Tunney landed with that terrific right, the fight was in the bag."

Incidentally, a similar British expression, *in the basket*, means exactly the opposite, that is, nothing doing, or rejected.

in the ballpark: *see* BALLPARK.

"In the long run we are all dead."
—Attributed to economist JOHN MAYNARD KEYNES

in the long run
Over the long term; ultimately. The term originated in racing, where it alludes to the competitor who may be off to a slow start but picks up speed and wins the race. At first sometimes put as *at the long run*, the term was transferred to more general use by the 17th century.

in the money: *see under* MONEY ...

in there pitching, to be
To exert one's best effort; to be actively trying. The term, which alludes to the baseball pitcher's pivotal role, began to be used figuratively about 1940. The *Saturday Evening Post* had it: "Everybody on the system is in there pitching, trying to save a locomotive or piece of locomotive" (June 26, 1943).

in the running, to be
To be among the leading competitors; to be eligible for a prize. The term comes from horse racing, where it simply means a horse that will compete (as opposed to one that is OUT OF THE RUNNING). It began to be transferred to other kinds of contest in the late 19th century. W. Somerset Maugham had it in *Cakes and Ale* (1930), writing about best-selling books: "At all events Edward Driffield is in the running."

in the same league, to be
To be in the same class; on the same level of expertise. This term alludes to the leagues of baseball clubs, categorized as major or minor (see also MAJOR LEAGUE; BUSH LEAGUE), which have been in existence since the late 19th century. The expression began to be used figuratively for other activities by the early 20th century. It is so used on both sides of the Atlantic. For example, a London *Times* item of Feb. 22, 1973,

has it, "The latest incident is not in the same league as the apparently endless series of espionage scandals in and around Bonn in 1968 and 1969" (cited by *OED*). A synonym for *not in the same league* is *out of one's league*, although the former tends to be in the context of downgrading ("the church choir is not in the same league as the Metropolitan Opera chorus") while the latter tends to be more neutral ("the prices in this restaurant are out of my league").

> *"His neighborhood is getting into the swim of the real-estate movement."*
>
> —*Harper's Magazine*, 1889

in the swim
Up to date; in the thick of the action. The term, of course, alludes to swimming, the oldest of water sports. Greek warriors swam for fitness, but the ancient Romans and the ancient Japanese both regarded it purely as a sport, holding competitive races as early as 36 B.C. The figurative use of the term dates from the second half of the 19th century, although it may on occasion have been used with a slightly different meaning. A *Macmillan's Magazine* issue from November, 1869, had, "A man is said to be 'in the swim' when any piece of good fortune has happened to him.... The metaphor is piscatorial." The writer of this item apparently thought that the expression alluded to a fish that escaped the angler's hook (hence the "piscatorial") and therefore was again swimming freely. Today the expression simply means active engagement in events.

> *"The voters are saying, 'In your face, Bush!' They are saying, 'In your face, Clinton!' That's because the voters are stressed out."*
>
> —RUSSELL BAKER, *New York Times*, June 6, 1992

in your face
Militantly challenging, rudely aggressive. This term comes from basketball, at least as it is played in rough playground games. (It may actually have originated as a reversal of "Get out of my

face," slang for "Get away from me" since at least 1930.) In basketball it refers to a blatant offensive display, such as executing a SLAM DUNK despite a close-guarding attempt by the defense. By 1988 it was being used figuratively for similar audacious aggressive maneuvers or behavior, as in "the in-your-face style of New York politics" that candidate Bill Clinton met with when campaigning on New York City streets (reported in the *New York Times*, cited by William Safire, May 31, 1992).

> *"Mel Hein, the great center-linebacker who was the iron man and captain of the Giants teams that won seven division titles and two league championships, died at his home in San Clemente."*
> —New York Times, Feb. 3, 1992

iron man

The strongest member of a group; the mainstay of an organization. This term already was being used figuratively in the 17th century, when it had no previous sports-connected origin but presumably alluded to the strength of iron. However, it was adopted into sports terminology in the 20th century. In baseball it tended to be applied only to pitchers who showed extraordinary stamina and power. In football and other sports it simply denoted a durable player who either plays every game or who has played every game for a team for a number of successive seasons. Its current figurative use most likely comes from sports. This usage was further reinforced from the late 1970's on through the name and increasing publicity for Hawaii's very difficult triathlon, the Iron Man (also Ironman). As *Sports Illustrated* described it, "The Iron Man contest was born when someone wondered what would happen if endurance tests in swimming, bicycling and running were piled on one another in a single event" (May 14, 1979). The contest combines a 2.4-mile swim, 112-mile bicycle race, and 26.2-mile road race.

it ain't over till it's over

Don't predict the outcome of an event until it is actually finished. The term here is attributed to baseball's highly quotable

Yogi Berra, who allegedly said it of the 1973 National League
pennant race, when the New York Mets bounced up and down
repeatedly before they finally won their division. It has been
stated slightly differently by other writers—for example, *the
game isn't over till it's over*—and Berra himself, who was Mets
manager at the time, once said *he* had actually been quoting
pitcher Bob Feller, who said, "When it is over, it is over."

it's a whole new ball game: *see* WHOLE NEW BALL GAME.

it's your ball/catch
It's up to you; it's in your hands. This baseball/football version
of the tennis term, the BALL'S IN YOUR COURT, is in Britain also
put as the *ball is with you*. All these locutions were transferred to general figurative use around the turn of the 20th
century and have become more and more common.

"At the beginning of the twentieth century, the Ivy League athlete who combined sporting proficiency with stiff character and the proper social credentials was a bona fide American hero."
—CHRISTIAN MESSENGER, *Journal of Popular Culture*, 1974/75

Ivy League

Describing a relatively exalted level of social prestige and scholastic achievement. It alludes to the colleges constituting the Ivy League, an athletic league founded in 1856. They include most of the oldest American colleges: Harvard, Yale, Princeton, Columbia, Dartmouth, Cornell, Brown, and the University of Pennsylvania. In the 1930's their reputation for academic excellence and social standing was transferred to their students and alumni; today, the term also implies a degree of snobbishness. The actual name Ivy League alludes to the ivy-covered walls of the school buildings.

jinx

A period of bad luck; a person or event that brings on bad luck. The origin of this Americanism of the early 20th century appears to be lost, but the word has been closely associated with baseball from that time. Paul Dickson quotes John B. Foster's 1908 definition of it: "another name for a ball player's superstitious ideas." Although some etymologists claim it is related to the wrynecked woodpecker, also called *jynx* and associated with witchcraft since the Middle Ages, there is no verification for this origin, and the earliest citations all are American. The *Chicago Daily News* had it in 1911: "Dave Shean and 'Peaches' Graham ... have not escaped the jinx that has been following the champions." It was being transferred to bad luck in nonathletic situations by the 1920's.

jock

An athlete; an individual deeply involved in sports and/or exercise; by extension, one whose self-image depends heavily on his or her athletic prowess. This word appears to have originated in America as a shortening of JOCKSTRAP and is used in an admiring or derogatory way, depending on both speaker and context. For example, in some colleges, students disparagingly call an introductory course in geology "rocks for jocks," implying it is an easy way to fulfill a science requirement for those more interested in sports than academics. Similarly, critics of male sexist attitudes sometimes identify jock with this kind of machismo.

The current American slang use of "jock" dates from the mid-20th century and has, during the fitness craze of recent decades, been extended to athletic women as well as men. In Britain "jock" also is used as an abbreviation for the noun "jockey," a usage seldom found in America.

"Racing, whatever else it inspires, certainly produces no indifference."

—JACK LEACH, *A Rider on the Stand* (1970)

jockey for position, to

To maneuver for an advantageous position. This expression is a straightforward transfer from the rider's attempts to obtain the most favorable position—on the rail—during a horse race. The verb *to jockey* used alone similarly means to operate or guide the movement of something, just as a rider guides a horse.

Racehorse riders have been called jockeys since the 17th century. The first woman jockey to ride a race was Alicia Meynell, in York in 1804; she was the mistress of the horse's owner. Today there are women jockeys, but they still constitute a minority; the first licensed woman jockey in the United States was Kathy Kusner (1968). Among the most famous jockeys of all time was the American Willie Shoemaker, who in 1935 became the first to win 400 races in a single year (he went on to win 485 races in 1953, an all-time record).

In the early 20th century the noun "jockey" began to be used in figurative fashion for other individuals who "drove" some kind of apparatus. Chiefly in America, such terms as *trolley jockey*, *truck jockey*, and *garage jockey* came into use. In the mid-20th century came the still more figurative term *disc jockey*, at first a radio broadcaster who conducts a show consisting of recorded music and announcements, interspersed with informal talk, and soon after one who selects and plays recorded music at a dance or discotheque.

> "You can enjoy perfect comfort and freedom. Schnoter's Suspensories and Jock Straps have gained their widespread popularity by quality, wear, fit and low price."
>
> —Advertisement, *The Billboard*, Dec. 20, 1919

jockstrap

An elasticized cloth belt worn to support and protect the male genitals. Originally used primarily for sports, it is listed by the U.S. Patent Office as an invention of Charles F. Bennett of Chicago in 1897. It can serve to keep in place a hard-surfaced protective cup, made of plastic or some other material, making it especially useful for contact sports. However, jockstraps also are worn by nonathletes under loose shorts, bathing trunks, and other garments, and by dancers under tights.

The name "jockstrap" is derived from the word *jock*, which in the late 18th century was rude slang for the male genitals. It was so listed in H. T. Potter's *New Dictionary of Cant and Flash* (c. 1790). Further, the 1796 edition of Francis Grose's *A Classical Dictionary of the Vulgar Tongue* has the entry "to jock," defined as "to enjoy a woman," with the notation that it was in use from 1690. Also see JOCK.

In 1990, Chicago White Sox player Steve Lyons slid headfirst into a base during a game at Detroit's Tiger Stadium and ended up with his pants full of dirt. Forgetting the crowd of 15,000 onlookers, he pulled down his pants and tried to brush the dirt off his legs, revealing his jockstrap not only to them but to the TV audience (a camera was trained on him at the time). Only the roar of laughter reminded him where he was, and he quickly pulled up his pants, but his mistake earned him a permanent chuckle in baseball history.

> *"Racing may begin earlier than the gun, but the start is when the cards come down."*
> —JOHN CHAMIER, *Small Boat and Dinghy Racing* (1963)

jump the gun, to

To begin prematurely or act too hastily. The expression alludes to the starter's gun that marks the beginning of a race, where someone who "jumps" the gun is starting before the gun has gone off. The term began life as *beat the pistol* but had changed to the current form by 1942, when it appeared in the *American Thesaurus of Slang.*

K K K K K

karate chop

A strong argument or other figurative blow against something or someone. In the years following World War II the Asian martial arts of judo and karate grew increasingly popular as both sports and methods of self-defense. Karate, whose name is based on the Japanese words for "empty" and "hands," relies on defending oneself by striking sensitive parts of an attacker's body with the hands, elbows, knees, and feet. One such movement, the chop, a sharp, slanting blow usually struck with the side of the hand, is particularly forceful and dramatic. About 1970 it began to be used figuratively for forceful arguments, as in "President Nixon's $200 billion budget . . . was a karate chop in the fight against inflation, but it will take time to see how well the blow was aimed" (*Tuscaloosa News*, Feb. 8, 1970).

keep the ball rolling, to

To keep an undertaking from flagging. This term appears to have come from the somewhat earlier *keep the ball up*, which was used figuratively in Britain from the late 18th century. Jeremy Bentham had it in a letter of 1781 to G. Wilson: "I put a word in now and then to keep the ball up." Presumably it came from one or another ball game—the *OED* lists it as such—but its precise origin has been lost. The current term began to be used in America a few decades later. Several authorities believe it gained impetus through the practice of rolling huge balls in political parades during the 1840 presidential campaign. Whatever its ultimate derivation, today it means to keep things going, as in "Certainly no one was better prepared to take an active part in urging the Yosemite grant and to keep the ball rolling" (*Sierra Club Bulletin*, March, 1948).

> *"We were forever being told 'Keep your eye on the ball.' "*
> —Screen Book (1907), cited by the *OED*

keep your eye on the ball
Stay alert; pay attention. The origin of this term is uncertain. A number of sports would qualify, especially baseball, cricket, and any of the racket sports, where players must watch the path of the ball carefully in order to hit it squarely (with bat or racket). It was being used figuratively by about 1900.

> *"The only thing I got right was a kickoff."*
> —Baseball pitcher DIZZY DEAN, on his attempt
> to broadcast a football game (1947)

kick off, to
To begin. Also *kickoff*, a beginning. This term, which was being transferred to any kind of starting action from the mid-19th century on, probably came first from soccer but is used in numerous other sports. In soccer a kickoff starts play at the beginning of each half and after a goal; it is place-kicked from the center spot with the players positioned in their own half of the field. In college football, a kickoff means to put the ball in play at the beginning of a game. Until 1912 it was delivered from midfield, which was then changed to the 40-yard line. In professional football, the ball is place-kicked at the start of each half and after every touchdown or field goal from the 35-yard line. Other games involving kickoffs are Australian Rules football, rugby, and speedball.

killer instinct
A drive to succeed. This term was first used figuratively in

the first half of the 20th century for boxers, although it may have been used more literally in earlier decades (probably by biologists describing particularly fierce animals). It appeared in a 1931 treatise on boxing in a description of Jack Dempsey: "He had more fighting spirit and more of the sheer killer instinct in him than was in all four of them rolled together" (cited by *OED*). It was later extended to other sports and still later to fighting spirit in any kind of competition.

> "He believed cataloguing to be the kingpin of the library system."
>
> —*Library Journal* (1895)

kingpin
The central or most important member of a group; the key element in a plan or system. The term comes from bowling, where the center or No. 5 pin has been called the kingpin since the late 18th century.

> "It was thinking of what you call consequences . . . that prevented me from . . . making it a real knock-down and drag-out."
>
> —JAMES FENIMORE COOPER, *The Prairie* (1827)

knock-down drag-out
A fierce battle, figurative or literal. This term, from free-for-all fisticuffs, has been around since the early 19th century and was being used figuratively within a few decades. Sometimes it was shortened to knock-down, as by Lewis Carroll in *Through the Looking Glass* (1872): "I meant 'there's a nice knock-down argument for you!'—But 'glory' doesn't mean 'a nice knock-down argument,' Alice objected.—When *I* use a word, Humpty Dumpty said, in a rather scornful tone, it means just what I choose it to mean—neither more nor less."

"To be knocked out doesn't mean what it seems. A boxer does not have to get up."

—JOYCE CAROL OATES, quoted by George
Vecsey, *New York Times*, Mar. 4, 1987

knockout

Very attractive; also, *k.o.*, *kayo*, *knockout blow*, a decisive or defeating action. This term comes from boxing, where it denotes the end of a fight, either because one contender is unable to recover from the last blow or because the officials have declared one fighter the winner (a *technical knockout*). As a decisive action or defeat, the term was being used figuratively by the 1890's. The colloquial usage of terming something or someone of surpassing attractiveness or quality a knockout dates from the same period.

knock the ball over the fence

A major success. This term, which in baseball means a home run—the best a batter can do—was transferred to other kinds of success in the second half of the 20th century. See also HOME RUN.

"Dope . . . a guy who doesn't know the score."

—D. NOWINSON, *Better English* (1938)

know the score, to

To understand what is really happening; to have inside knowledge. The ultimate origin of the literal use of this phrase is not recorded. The word "score" has meant the tally of points won or lost in games and sports since the 15th century. The figurative use of the term, however, dates only from the first half of the 20th century. Dizzy Dean, the colorful St. Louis Cardinals pitcher of the 1930's who became almost as famous for his malapropisms as Yogi Berra, was quoted as saying, after a 1–0 game, "The game was closer than the score indicated" (by George F. Will, *Men at Work*, 1990). Also see SCORE.

late inning

Approaching the end of any proceeding. The term comes from baseball, where it means the eighth or ninth inning, nearing the end of the game. In the second half of the 20th century it has been occasionally transferred to other enterprises, as in "Nearing the Christmas break, it was a late inning in the semester."

lateral pass

A sidetracking maneuver. The term comes from football, where it designates a throw in any direction except toward the opponent's goal line. Thrown either to the side or backward, it can be used behind the line of scrimmage or when the ball-carrier has passed the line of scrimmage and wants to give possession of the ball to a teammate. It is occasionally used figuratively, as in "The candidate threw the reporter a lateral pass, answering his pointed questions with the standard party line."

lead the field, to

To be ahead of everyone else in some endeavor. The term appears to have originated in hunting, alluding to the pursuing hounds, but also was used in early horse racing. It dates from approximately 1800. A related expression from hunting is *leader of the pack*, referring to the leader of the hounds chasing a fox. It, too, is used figuratively, for the foremost individual in a group or enterprise.

> "If you are going to 'lead freely,' you have got to 'take punishment,' if you will allow me to speak in the language of those who box."
> —THEODORE ROOSEVELT, *Works*, 1895

lead with one's chin, to

To take a risk; to behave incautiously. The term comes from

boxing, where it literally means leaving the chin unprotected against the opponent's blows. It began to be transferred in the first half of the 20th century. Mystery writer Erle Stanley Gardner had it in a short story: "Let him lead with *his* chin" (*Argosy*, Apr., 1949; cited by *OED*).

> *"In everything but natural gifts, he had so much start that I was left at the post."*
> —C. P. SNOW, *The Conscience of the Rich* (1958)

left at the post

Left behind. The post alluded to here is the one marking the starting point of a horse race (the *starting post*), and a horse left there is one that is slow to start. The term began to be used figuratively for any kind of slow starter in the first half of the 20th century. (The word *post* has another racetrack meaning as well, that is, the outside lane, which is the least advantageous, but that sense is not intended in this idiom.)

left field: *see* OUT IN LEFT FIELD.

left hook

A powerful blow delivered on a curve. The term comes from boxing, where it describes an important part of a prizefighter's arsenal: a short punch delivered in an arc by the left fist, with the elbow bent. The brief 1991 Persian Gulf War to liberate Kuwait from its Iraqi invaders was virtually ended in one day by a maneuver in which a ground force moved from the Allied line in Saudi Arabia and made a large arc to reach the back of the Iraqi lines. This maneuver was called a HAIL MARY by commanding General H. Norman Schwartzkopf but is perhaps more accurately described as *the great left hook maneuver*, the term used by his biographers, Roger Cohen and Claudio Gatti (according to a *New York Times* book review by James Blackwell, Sept. 5, 1991).

*"She was now devoting all her energies to giving them
a leg up."*

—W. E. NORRIS, *Misadventure* (1890)

leg up, (give someone) a

To help; to give someone a boost. The term comes from riding,
where it refers to a person clasping both hands together to
form a kind of stirrup to help another person mount a horse.
The term was being used figuratively in Britain in the first
half of the 19th century but apparently did not cross the Atlantic for another century. It appeared in print in the *Topeka
Journal* in 1940 (cited in *American Speech*).

let the side down, to

To fail to support, or to disappoint one's colleagues. This term
originated in Britain and in all likelihood comes from cricket,
rugby, or another team sport, for the British tend to call a
team a "side." Although it is still more commonly used in
Britain, the expression is also heard in North America.

level playing field, a

Equal terms, par. This term comes from Britain, where in
such popular sports as cricket and lawn bowls an even-
surfaced field makes a considerable difference. It began to be
used figuratively in America to mean equal conditions, or par,
in the latter half of the 20th century. For example, the *Atlanta Constitution*, reporting on the passage of a law deregu-
lating depository institutions in May, 1981, had it: "The
legislation ... will, in theory and somewhat in practice, put
banks and S&Ls on an equal legal and business basis—a 'level
playing field' is the description often used."

lightweight

Unimportant, small-time. This term is used in boxing and
horse racing, as well as some other sports. In boxing it denotes the 135-pound weight division (139 pounds for amateurs). In racing, it may mean either a horse carrying a light
weight or a jockey riding at a low weight. In both sports the

terms have been around since the 18th century, and they were
being used figuratively for individuals or things of little con-
sequence by 1800 or so.

line of scrimmage

The point of contention between two sides. The term has been
used since about 1900 in football, where it designates an imaginary line where the ball is placed at the end of each play, and
on either side of which the teams line up, facing each other.
Neither team may cross the line of scrimmage until the center
snaps the ball—that is, puts it in play by passing it from the
ground backward between his legs to a back behind him. William Safire used the term incorrectly in a political piece he
wrote but corrected himself in a later column on language, indicating he should have said: "We righties come to our side of
the line of scrimmage with different mental sets" (*New York
Times*, October, 1990).

> *"All right, everyone, line up alphabetically according
> to your height."*
>
> —CASEY STENGEL, New York Yankees manager

lineup

A number of persons, things, or events arranged in a particular order for an activity, inspection, etc. The term originated
in the mid-19th century in baseball, where it designates the
list of players participating in a game and the positions they
will play. By 1900 it was being used figuratively on both sides
of the Atlantic for any such list, as in "The Celebrity Series
announced a star-studded lineup for next season's concerts."

little old lady in tennis shoes

A conventional, unsophisticated, middle-class, middle-aged or
elderly woman who doesn't care about fashion. This Americanism was born in the 1920's. Many think it is an elaboration
of a statement made by the legendary editor Harold Ross in
1925: "The *New Yorker* will not be edited for the [little] old
lady from Dubuque." Ross was alluding to the sophistication
his magazine aspired to. Exactly who added the tennis shoes,
with their implication of tacky unfashionableness, is not

known. In the 1970's, when tennis shoes or sneakers—now generally called *athletic shoes*—became at first fashionable and soon afterward the basic footwear of everyday American life, the expression's literal meaning underwent a radical change. However, figuratively it is still used in the same disparaging way, often by the lady herself.

> *"One of 'em's always got their mind on their crotch.*
> *—I appreciate the locker room wisdom. I'll take it*
> *under advisement."*
>
> —TOM KAKONIS, *Double Down* (1991)

locker-room

Raunchy, sexually explicit, and/or smelly. The term, of course, is a descriptive extension from the actual locker rooms used by sports teams, alluding to the type of conversation and jokes often found there. Although by the late 20th century the numbers of women athletes had grown exponentially, the term still refers to an all-male bastion. It became a more general adjective about the mid-20th century.

> *"He was going too fast by a long shot."*
>
> —J. R. BARTLETT, *Americanisms* (1848)

long shot, a

A slim chance of success. This term originated in the 18th century and probably alluded to the inaccuracy of firearms, in warfare as well as the sport of target shooting. However, it became closely associated with horse racing, where it refers to a bet on an unlikely horse and consequently paying *long odds* if it does win. It was being transferred to other kinds of unlikelihood by the early 19th century and remains current, especially in the locution *not by a long shot*, meaning highly unlikely.

loser: *see* GOOD LOSER.

Lou Gehrig's disease
Amyotrophic lateral sclerosis. This wasting neurological disorder still has no specific treatment or cure and ends in death. It was not very well known when Lou Gehrig, an outstanding first baseman for the New York Yankees, playing in a record 2,130 consecutive games (1925–1939), was forced to retire because the disease had begun to ruin his coordination and sap his strength. Gehrig was not only a fine fielder and batter—he won the American League home-run championship three times, hit 493 homers in his career, and had a lifetime batting average of .340—but he played even when exhausted, ill, or injured. Nicknamed the Iron Horse, he was never as famous in life as his teammate Babe Ruth, but his name became permanently attached to the disease that killed him in 1941, at the age of 38.

low blow
An unfair, unexpected attack. The term comes from boxing, where it means hitting BELOW THE BELT. Normally the boxer doing so will be penalized by the loss of points or be disqualified from the bout. Used figuratively since the mid-20th century, the expression no doubt became popular because of its rhyme.

lucky break
Unexpected good fortune. This term probably comes from billiards, where "break" has meant a consecutive series of suc-

cessful strokes since the mid-19th century. However, a similar phrase was used as early as 1827 by John Randolph: "I am of opinion that (as we say in Virginia) we have made a 'great break.' In fact, the administration have succeeded in no one measure" (letter to Dr. Brockenburgh, published in *Life*, 1851).

M M M M M

magic number

The atomic number or neutron number of exceptionally stable protons or neutrons. This term has been used by physicists since the 1940's and may simply have been invented for the situation it describes. However, it also may have come from one of several American team sports, where it designates a number representing the combination of victories for a leading team and losses for its close opponents that will guarantee the leader's winning a league championship. In baseball, for example, suppose the Boston Red Sox, in first place in the American League East, have a two-game lead over the New York Yankees and four games remain to be played. The Red Sox magic number is 3, for three wins by them, three losses for the Yankees, or any combination of Red Sox wins and Yankee losses that total 3 will mean that the Yankees cannot finish ahead of the Red Sox. In ice hockey, league standings are computed in points, a team receiving 2 points for a victory or 1 point for a tied game. Therefore the "magic number" refers to the number of points a team must gain in order to win the league championship.

main event

The most important of several occurrences, agenda items, performances, or issues. The term comes from boxing, where since the turn of the 20th century it has denoted the most important bout of several being presented in one evening. It began to be used figuratively for the main attraction, at first just for performances (vaudeville shows, circuses, etc.) but later for other kinds of enterprise as well.

"They intended to compete in the major league and they knew that if the company were to survive it had to . . . meet any competition."

—G. AMBERG, *Ballet* (1949)

major league
Imposing, top-level. The term comes from baseball, where it designates the two principal American professional leagues, the American and the National. The National League is the older of the two, founded as the National Association in 1871. After many rival leagues had been formed and had failed, the American League was organized in 1900. The National at first did not recognize the newcomer, but by 1903 most of the differences between the two had been settled and the first series between their pennant winners was played that year.

The term "major league," which distinguishes these top-level baseball organizations from lesser professional leagues (see MINOR LEAGUE; BUSH LEAGUE), then began to be used figuratively for the top level of any sports enterprise or competition. Later it was extended to anyone or anything belonging to the most important or best or largest of its kind, so that we speak of, for example, a major-league violinist, major-league computer program, or major-league choral society. Writing about a poker game in his 1991 novel, *Double Down*, Tom Kakonis had it: "An' this A-rab comin' in, you say he's major-league?" A synonym is BIG LEAGUE.

major player: *see* PLAYER.

make the cut, (not) to
To be chosen (or fail to be chosen) in an elimination process, as for the cast of a play, a sales force sent overseas, etc. The term comes from football, where it means to survive the elimination of unneeded or less able players from the team or roster. Among the most famous players cut by National Football League teams over the years was Johnny Unitas, nicknamed the "Cinderella Man." Never an outstanding quarterback in college or in semiprofessional play, he was a Steeler rookie in

1955 and was cut in training camp. He hitchhiked home to Pittsburgh and played for the semiprofessional Bloomfield Rams, two games a week for $6 a game. Early the following year he was signed by the Baltimore Colts as a second-string quarterback. During one game he was called in to replace the regular quarterback, who had been injured, and it became clear that he would be the regular quarterback from then on. During his eighteen-year career, Unitas amassed a total of more than 40,000 yards of passes (exceeded only by Fran Tarkenton), as well as a record of touchdown passes in 47 consecutive games—nearly twice as long a streak as any quarterback in history.

marathon

Any event of long duration. This term has an ancient origin— the battle of Marathon in 490 B.C., whose outcome was reported to Athens by a runner who ran some 26 miles to do so. However, today it is closely associated with sports, because the name was used for a long-distance foot race in the 1896 Olympic Games, the first revival of the ancient Greek games. In 1908 a standard distance for this race was set, 42 kilometers, 52 meters (26 miles, 385 yards), which is still used for other foot races bearing the name marathon (Boston Marathon, run every spring on Patriots' Day; New York Marathon; etc.). In other sports the name is used for long-distance races of a different length, for example, an 18-mile swim in open water or a horse race longer than 1.25 miles.

By 1920 the name had been extended to other events. It was used for dance contests (*dance marathon*) in which couples continuously danced in a ballroom as long as they could—as much as 48 hours in some instances. Still later it was extended to other events of exceptional length or requiring exceptional endurance, such as a *sales marathon*.

"These messengers from paradise are mascots, my friends; happy is he to whom heaven gives a mascot."
—EDMOND AUDRAN, *La Mascotte* (1880)

mascot

A good-luck charm consisting of an object, animal, or person. Although this word first gained currency as the title of Audran's opera (quoted above), with a libretto by Duru and Chivot, it quickly became associated with sports. In baseball in the late 19th century it designated a bat boy or person who did odd jobs for the players and who wore a team uniform. In football it attached itself to the Yale bulldog, Handsome Dan, owned by one of the members of the class of 1892, and in professional football to a Skye terrier serving as Pittsburgh's good-luck charm. Probably because athletes often are somewhat superstitious about what helps them win or lose—a particular tennis skirt, touching one's baseball cap in a certain way, etc.—mascots tend to appeal to them. Indeed, more and more elaborate items served as mascots for racing-car drivers, so that in 1955 *Halsbury's Statutory Instruments* included the rule: "No mascot shall be carried by a motor vehicle ... where it is likely to strike any person with whom the vehicle may collide."

meal ticket

Any individual, object, or quality that guarantees success. Literally, of course, a meal ticket first (late 19th century) was a ticket entitling its holder to a meal. However, the term was quickly transferred to anyone or anything that provided someone with income or success, and was widely used in sports. In baseball it meant a consistently excellent player, especially a good pitcher. In the 1930's Carl Hubbell of the New York Giants was nicknamed "King Carl the Meal Ticket"; his efforts resulted in winning 115 games from 1933 to 1937.

"Many men, who shine in the minor leagues, fail to make good in the majors."

—CHRISTY MATHEWSON, *Pitching* (1912)

minor league

Low-level, of little importance. The term comes from baseball, where it denotes any professional U.S. or Canadian league other than the two major leagues (see MAJOR LEAGUE). In 1990 there were approximately sixteen minor leagues, designated AAA, AA, A, or Rookie. The expression was being transferred to other endeavors by the mid-20th century, so that one speaks, for example, of a minor-league orchestra, minor-league talent, or minor-league brand of ketchup.

miscue

An error resulting in failure. The term comes from billiards, where since the second half of the 19th century it has meant failing to strike the ball properly with the cue. It was being transferred to other kinds of mistake by the 1880's.

"If I mysse nat my marke, he is a busy felowe."

—JEHAN PALSGRAVE, *La Langue Françoyse* (1530)

miss the mark, to

To miss the point; to get it wrong. This term, which originated in archery (like its close relative, HIT THE MARK), was being used figuratively for other kinds of error by the 16th century. Its synonym, *wide of the mark*, used perhaps more in Britain than in America, is also very old and was used figuratively in the 16th century by Shakespeare, among others. Indeed, it was so well known by 1678 that John Ray's *English Proverbs* of that year abbreviated it to "wide" ("Wide quoth Wilson").

A related British term, *off the mark*, may also have originated in archery but is now closely associated with cricket, where it means off to a start, that is, making your first run after coming to bat. From it comes *slow off the mark*, used figuratively for describing someone who is slow on the uptake.

> *"Bullfighting is worthless without rivalry. But with two great bullfighters it becomes a deadly rivalry."*
> —ERNEST HEMINGWAY, *Dangerous Summer* (1985)

moment of truth

The crucial point, when one is put to the ultimate test. The term comes from bullfighting and is a translation of the Spanish *el momento de la verdad*, the moment when the matador is about to kill the bull. It was first used in English in Ernest Hemingway's short story about bullfighting, *Death in the Afternoon*, and later was transferred to other critical junctures. The *Yale Law Journal* had it in 1962: "Finally, in the moment of truth, the judiciary has a telling advantage over the other branches, the prerogative of interpreting the Constitution."

> *"It was Monday morning, and all the Monday-morning quarterbacks were out. Or at least one of them. His name was Lieutenant Peter Byrnes, and he was telling his assembled detectives what he hoped they should have known by now."*
> —ED MCBAIN, *Widows* (1991)

Monday-morning quarterback

One who second-guesses or offers counsel about matters with which he or she is neither concerned nor well informed. The term refers to the after-the-fact football spectator who "knows" just how the quarterback could have won the game of the past weekend, or won with a higher score. An Americanism, the term originated about 1940 and soon was transferred to other examples of twenty-twenty hindsight. However, it is interesting to note that the 1911 edition of Ambrose Bierce's *The Devil's Dictionary* defined Monday as "In Christian countries, the day after the baseball game."

money, to finish in/out of the

To win/lose, or succeed/fail. The term comes from betting on horse races, where "money" signifies the first three finishers in a race for betting payoffs (the first four for distributing prize money). The terms were being used figuratively by about 1900.

mop/wipe the floor with, to

To defeat overwhelmingly. The term originally was boxing slang, hyperbole for a complete defeat, and was being used figuratively for other kinds of defeat by about 1900.

morning glory

An individual whose performance begins brilliantly but gradually deteriorates. The original reference is to the morning glory, a flower that blooms in the morning and wilts in the course of the day. In the late 19th century it became American baseball slang for a hitter who shines early in the season or a rookie who is off to a fine start but never fulfills his early promise. About the mid-20th century it was transferred to other individuals or proceedings showing promise at first but becoming lackluster with time.

Most Valuable Player: *see* MVP.

> "*The moves he threw (and he'd rehearsed them in his head a hundred times: slow motion, fast forward, freeze frame, the whole screening) were going to have to be his best ones.*"
>
> —TOM KAKONIS, *Crisscross* (1990)

move, a

A deceptive maneuver. This American slang expression comes from several sports. In track or other kinds of racing, it signifies a maneuver that ends in overtaking the leader, as in "She began her move on the next-to-last lap." In basketball it signifies a deceptive movement or fake, as in "He put a move on his man and lost him."

"These conditions are clear-cut and are not open to reinterpretation, and I do not believe in moving the goalposts."

—GEORGE BUSH, press conference, 1990

move the goalposts, to
To change the rules or terms after a conflict or contest has begun. This term presumably alludes to the goalposts used in sports—hockey, football, etc.—and began to be used figuratively for midstream rules changes about 1970. President Bush, in the quotation above, was explaining his criteria for opening trade with South Africa (according to William Safire, *New York Times*, Oct. 28, 1990).

"In 1986, armed with old-fashioned moxie . . . she [Linda J. Wachner] led a $550 million hostile takeover of Warnaco, Inc., a sleepy, flabby maker of lingerie and men's sportswear, badly in need of overhaul.

—STEPHANIE STROM, *New York Times*, May 17, 1992

moxie
Nerve and skill. This term comes from Moxie, the trade name of a soft drink that was created in 1876 and originally marketed as a "nerve tonic." The noncapitalized "moxie" took its meaning from the "nerve" part of the advertised claim and was first used for athletes, particularly baseball players, who showed exceptional mettle in a tight situation. It was being transferred to nonathletes from about 1930 on.

muff, to
To bungle, to perform clumsily. This term comes from baseball. In the 1860's the word *muffin* was used for an unskilled player. (Possibly the original allusion was to dropping a ball like a hot muffin.) Poor playing was called *muffinism*, and a fielding error was called a *muff*. The verb form developed from these and eventually was transferred to making any kind of error.

muscle-bound

Rigid, inflexible. The term comes from bodybuilding, where overexercise can result in overdeveloped, bunched muscles that lead to inflexibility and poor coordination. It dates from about 1870 and was being transferred to other kinds of inflexibility by about 1915.

muscle man

A bodyguard, a person employed for his physical strength. This term, too, originally referred only to individuals devoted to bodybuilding exercises, or to those with a brawny build that looked as if it resulted from this pursuit. In the 1920's it began to be used figuratively for "enforcers," that is, those

who used or threatened violence on behalf of their criminal
employers, and later simply for any kind of bodyguard.

MVP

A key performer in any field. The term is an abbreviation for
the Most Valuable Player of baseball (and later football, too).
In baseball it originated as the Chalmers award in 1911, a
Chalmers automobile being given to the outstanding player in
each league. The first National League winner was Frank
Schulte of the Chicago Cubs; the first American League winner was Ty Cobb of the Detroit Tigers. The award ended in
1914 but was reinstated in the American League after the
1922 season and in the National League after 1924. Since 1931
the winners have been chosen by the Baseball Writers' Association. Among the few players who have been chosen three
times are Mike Schmidt (National League) and Jimmy Foxx,
Joe DiMaggio, Yogi Berra, Mickey Mantle, and Roger
Clemens (American League). Some omissions for this honor
have been rather curious. In 1942 and again in 1947 Ted Williams of the Boston Red Sox led the American League in batting, home runs, and runs batted in—the so-called triple
crown—but in both years he failed to win the MVP award,
probably because he did not get along well with many sportswriters. In 1946, however, he did win it, even though in that
year he finished second in batting, homers, and RBIs.

In football, the MVP award, established in 1955, is officially called the Jim Thorpe Trophy and is chosen in a poll of
National Football League players. The first such award went
to Harlon Hill of the Chicago Bears. The only three-time winner to date has been Earl Campbell of the Houston Oilers. In
basketball, the National Basketball Association MVP award
has been given since 1956. The only five-time winner to date
is Kareem Abdul-Jabbar, and Wilt Chamberlain won it four
times.

name of the game, the

The ultimate goal; the crux of the matter. The origin of this term has been lost, but it seems safe to assume it comes from sports and first referred to some essential aspect, such as "Returning your opponent's serve is the name of the game." It was being used figuratively from about 1960 and has been applied to just about any situation, as, for example, "Conserving our wetlands—that's the name of the game."

> "It's late in the day, and a neck and neck thing."
> —MORTIMER COLLINS, *Marquis and Merchant* (1871)

neck and neck

A close contest. The term comes from horse racing, where two horses in close competition appear to be running neck against neck. Used literally since about 1800, it was being transferred to other kinds of competition by 1810 or so.

neutral corner, in a

Not taking sides. The term refers to the boxing ring, where it means either of the two corners not being used by the boxers or their seconds. When a boxer knocks down his opponent, he must retire to a neutral corner until he is instructed to continue. The term has been around since the mid-20th century and was soon being transferred to other kinds of neutrality.

never change a winning game

Don't alter a successful course of action. Although the idea is scarcely new, the person most closely associated with this particular statement of it is tennis champion Bill Tilden, who in 1920 became the first American to win Wimbledon and in that same year won the first of six successive U.S. championships. In all, Tilden won three Wimbledon and seven U.S. singles titles and played on seven victorious U.S. Davis Cup teams. In a 1950 Associated Press poll that picked the best performer of the half-century in each sport, Tilden won in tennis by a greater margin than Babe Ruth in baseball, Red Grange in football, Jack Dempsey in boxing, and Bobby Jones in golf. He also wrote four tennis-instruction books that still are among the best of their kind. Although the style of playing has changed considerably since his death in 1953, Tilden's advice on tactics remains valid. "Tennis is essentially a game of brains," he maintained, "and matches are won by the men who use their brains to direct their shots." His most famous rule was "Never change a winning game; always change a losing game." It has been quoted by coaches in just about every sport, as well as transferred to general usage.

new ball game: *see* WHOLE NEW BALL GAME.

> *"I warrant you, thei can make it more nice than wise."*
> —BARNABY RICH, *Farewell to the Militarie Profession* (1581)

nice guys finish last

Ruthless tactics succeed more than kindness. This statement is generally ascribed to baseball manager Leo Durocher, whose fiery style earned him the nickname "The Lip." Colorful and outspoken to his players and infuriating to opposing teams, he played for seventeen seasons, mostly as shortstop, but it was as manager that he made his name. He led three teams into the World Series—the 1941 Brooklyn Dodgers, who lost to the New York Yankees; the 1951 New York Giants, who lost to the Yankees; and the 1954 Giants, who swept the Cleveland Indians. Despite his much quoted dictum, which was allegedly his response in 1946 when asked about the Giants' chances, Durocher did end up last once, in 1966, his first season with the Chicago Cubs (they went 59–103, but the following year they improved to 87–74).

The idea behind Durocher's statement is, of course, an ancient one. "More nice than wise" had made it into John

Ray's proverb collection of 1670 and was often repeated. However, it is Durocher's version that took hold in the 20th century. Paul Gardner used it as the title of his book, *Nice Guys Finish Last: Sport and American Life* (1974).

> *"I would hope that understanding and reconciliation are not limited to the nineteenth hole alone."*
>
> —GERALD R. FORD

nineteenth hole

A convivial gathering place, especially a bar. The term comes from golf, where it denotes the clubhouse bar (the course itself, of course, consists of eighteen holes). However, it is occasionally used for an extra hole played to decide a tied round, that is, a single sudden-death hole (see also SUDDEN DEATH). The statement quoted above was made by President Ford, an avid golfer, at the dedication of the World Golf Hall of Fame (quoted in *New York Times*, Sept. 12, 1974), and alluded to the general atmosphere of good fellowship in a clubhouse bar, no matter how fierce the foregoing competition had been. The term originated about 1900.

ninth-inning rally

Last-minute revival of a dying cause, a failing enterprise, etc. The term comes from baseball, where it alludes to the rally of a team that is behind and surges ahead to win at virtually the last possible moment. Among the famous ninth-inning rallies in baseball history was that of the New York Giants in the 1951 pennant race. The Giants came back from 13 1/2 games behind the Brooklyn Dodgers on August 11 to force a three-game playoff. After splitting the first two games, Bobby Thomson hit a ninth-inning home run—"the shot heard round the world," some sportswriters called it—and the team won the pennant (but then lost the World Series to the New York Yankees).

no harm, no foul

An accident or potential disaster where no injury actually occurs. The term was coined by Los Angeles Lakers broadcaster Chick Hearn. In basketball it designates a foul that is
unimportant because no injury occurred and no advantage
was gained, and therefore the officials rule that play may continue. In the late 20th century it began to be transferred to
other situations, such as "The car skidded and went up over
the curb, but no harm, no foul."

no holds barred

Without any restrictions. The term is believed to come from
wrestling, where normally certain holds are not permitted. It
came into general use about 1940 and has since been applied
to just about any situation, as in "With deregulation, banks
will be able to enter the brokerage business on a no-holds-
barred basis."

> *"No gaine without pain."*
> —LEONARD WRIGHT, *Display of Dutie* (1589)

no pain, no gain

You must suffer in order to progress. This dictum, long uttered by athletic coaches urging players to train harder, is far
more ancient than most of them probably realize. Indeed,
"Without pains, no gains" was in John Ray's proverb collection of 1670, and some versions reinforce it by adding, "No
sweat, no sweet." Modern physical therapists, especially those
who help rehabilitate athletes after injury, dispute the truth
of the saying and insist that it is just such overdoing that
causes injury in the first place. Nevertheless, many exercise
addicts believe it, and it has been transferred to other enterprises as well.

no runs, no hits, no errors

Dull; faultless but uninteresting. The term comes from base-

ball and describes either an inning or an entire game in which
neither team makes any mistakes but also fails to score any
hits. A game without hits or errors can be (and has been) won
by means of a series of walks, provided at least one of them
scores a run. However, it can be boring for the spectators, at
least until suspense mounts toward the very end. Consequently the term is occasionally transferred to individuals or
situations that are essentially innocent or harmless but lackluster.

no skin off my nose

No concern of mine. This American slang expression from the
early 20th century is believed to come from boxing, although
that origin is sometimes disputed. It remains current, as in
"The service station went out of business, but it's no skin off
my nose."

not a Chinaman's chance

A very poor chance; practically no chance at all. Although
many authorities believe this expression originally alluded to
the poor prospects of Chinese miners during the 1840's Gold
Rush in the American West, where they were relegated to
the leftover tailings and had little or no chance of finding ore,
at least one writer believes differently. Paul Dickson maintains that the term came from a light-hitting boxer of the
1820's, Tom Spring, who was very likely to break down during
a long fight. He consequently was described as a "China
man," that is, as fragile as porcelain, and his small chances of
winning were later transferred to other kinds of dim prospect.
True or not, the theory is intriguing enough to warrant mention in this book.

not cricket
Unfair, unsportsmanlike. Cricket, Britain's national sport, has
become synonymous there with upright, gentlemanly behavior, and this expression originated there in the mid-19th century. Curiously enough, the term crossed the Atlantic even
though the sport itself baffles most Americans (and is only
slightly better known in Canada).

not in one's league: *see* IN THE SAME LEAGUE.

oddball

Eccentric, unusual, peculiar. Although this Americanism became current only about 1940, its precise origin has been lost. Because it obviously alludes to the eccentric path of a ball that is pitched or hit, it seems safe to assume that it comes from sports. While ball players may not have been the first to whom this sobriquet was attached, they are no more exempt from it than any other species of eccentric.

odds-on favorite

The one considered most likely to win. The term comes from racing, where the *odds* signifies the ratio of the amount one can win to the amount one risks in backing a particular horse. The odds, listed on a tote board, are determined by the total amount being wagered. As betting progresses the odds change constantly to reflect this activity. The higher the proportion of the total that is bet on a particular horse, the lower the odds will be. Therefore the odds-on favorite—the horse most people are betting will win—will actually pay off less, sometimes even less than the amount wagered (4–5, for example). This aspect of the term, however, is generally not transferred when it is used in a more general way to mean the overwhelming favorite in any sort of contest.

> "After I said some things like that, Casey [Stengel] was off and running again."
>
> —YOGI BERRA, *It Ain't Over* (1989)

off and running

Making a good start. The term comes from horse racing, where the announcer traditionally says, at the beginning of a race, "They're off [and running]." The statement doesn't make a great deal of sense, for if horses weren't doing so there would be no race at all. Nevertheless, the expression began to be used figuratively in the second half of the 20th century, as in the quotation above, which refers to Stengel's nonstop commentary.

off base
Mistaken, based on the wrong premise. The term comes from baseball, where it signifies a runner stepping off the base and therefore in a position to be put out. It was being used figuratively from about 1940 on. A very similar expression, to be *off one's base*, once meant (late 19th century) to be crazy, but it is seldom used today.

offside
In dubious taste, risqué. This term comes from football, field hockey, and ice hockey, where it denotes being in illegal territory. In rugby and soccer, however, a player is not penalized for being offside provided he or she is not seeking an advantage or scoring.

> "Oh, you who've been a-fishing will
>   indorse me when I say
> That it always is the biggest fish
>   you catch that gets away!"
>   —EUGENE FIELD, *Our Biggest Fish* (1892)

off the hook
Out of trouble; can't be blamed for something. The term comes from fishing and alludes to the fish that somehow manages to free itself from the hook and get away. From the 16th to 19th centuries, to be *off the hooks* meant to be crazy, or off one's head, but this usage is obsolete.

off the mark: *see* MISS THE MARK.

off the wall
Unconventional, bizarre. This bit of 20th-century American slang may come from racquetball or squash, where the ball can bounce off the wall in a weird way, or even from surfing,

where a large wave, called a wall, can break so as to send the surfer in a strange direction. The ball allusion seems the more likely one, but neither has been verified. Nevertheless, the term has been used to describe almost any sort of oddity since the late 1960's, as in "He's always asking off-the-wall questions."

old college try, (let's give it) the
Any strenuous effort. The expression, an Americanism used since the early 20th century, appears to have originated in collegiate team sports of one kind or another, where the coach or team captain exhorts the players to do their best. In baseball it was transferred to any desperate attempt to make a play— for example, going after a fly ball with only the remotest chance of catching it. Today it tends to be used ironically, as in "We haven't a prayer of finishing in time, but let's give it the old college try."

Olympic-size
The dimensions, distance, or other specifications prescribed for the Olympic Games or some other major athletic competition. The term is most often used to describe a swimming pool 50 meters (55 yards) long and at least 21 meters (23 yards) wide. It is also used for other athletic facilities, such as skating rinks.

The modern Olympic Games, modeled after the ancient Greek games, began to be held every four years in 1896. The Greeks, incidentally, used the word *Olympiad* to designate a four-year period reckoned from one Olympic Game to the next, beginning with the year 776 B.C. The same word today is used not only for the Olympic Games but for other competitions held at regular intervals, although not necessarily every four years. There is, for example, a World Chess Olympiad, held every two years.

on deck, to be
To be next in line, or on the agenda; to be ready for action. This term was originally nautical and referred to the main

deck of a ship but was taken over in several sports. In baseball it has meant, since the 1860's, to be next at bat, and the
on-deck circle is the area between the dugout (or bench) and
home plate, where the next batter waits his or her turn. In
various kinds of race—swimming, track, etc.—it means the
next to race among those waiting to compete. Mark Twain
was one of the first to use it figuratively, "Angels are always
on deck when there is a miracle to the fore" (*A Connecticut
Yankee in King Arthur's Court*, 1889; cited by *OED*).

> "*He was not in a one-on-one confrontation. There
> were a goodly array . . . of small fry present.*"
> —EMMA LATHEN, *Sweet and Low* (1974)

one-on-one
The interaction of two individuals; a direct encounter between
two persons. The term is used in several sports. In basketball
it signifies an informal game with just two players, as well as
the standard form of defense, in which one player guards one
opponent. In football it designates a situation in which a
player is covering, or is covered by, a single opponent; the latter is also called *man-to-man*. Writing about the 1960's, John
Madden had the latter, "In those years most teams used man-
to-man defenses against the pass, not the zone defenses they
went to later." It began to be transferred to nonathletic applications in the 1960's, as in "Bob doesn't enjoy double dating;
he prefers a one-on-one situation."

one that got away, the
The opponent who eluded you. The term comes from fishing,
where in the traditional FISH STORY the fish that escaped was
quite the biggest the angler had ever encountered. See also
OFF THE HOOK (and the quotation there).

one-two
A two-step or twofold combination that is strong and effective. The term comes from the *one-two punch* of boxing,
which consists of a short left jab followed immediately by a

hard right cross, usually to the jaw. The term is also used in fencing for an attack consisting of a fake disengage to draw a parry, followed by a thrust in the original line of engagement. The boxing term, which dates from about 1800, began to be used figuratively in the mid-20th century, as in "The new agency has proposed an excellent one-two combination of print and television ads."

"If he just watched out and kept on his toes, he'd be sure to get it."

—JOHN DOS PASSOS, *Three Soldiers* (1921)

on one's toes, to be
To be alert, ready for action. This term presumably comes from boxing, since a fighter must be on his toes in order to move fast and maneuver properly. The same would be true of a runner preparing to start a race. It began to be used figuratively in the early 20th century and then became even better known as the title of a highly successful musical comedy by Richard Rodgers and Lorenz Hart, *On Your Toes*, produced on Broadway in 1936 and made into a motion picture in 1939.

"If your broker does not know this, you had better get a broker who is on the ball."

—D. R. STARRETT, note to stockholders of the L. S. Starrett Company (1992)

on the ball, to be/have something
To be alert, clever, at one's best. This term was originally American and came from baseball, where it referred to a pitched ball with "something" on it—that is, spin or a curve. A pitcher who was working well was said to have something on the ball, which in the early 1900's was transferred to any individual who was doing something well. The expression has slightly different meanings in other sports. In soccer a player in possession of the ball is said to be on the ball. In Australian rules football it means playing in a ruck position so as to be al-

lowed to follow the ball anywhere in the field of play (a ruck is a group of players, including a rover and three followers, who are free to play all over the field, whereas their teammates must stay in fairly fixed positions).

on the button
On the exact spot. This term comes from boxing, where "button" has signified the point of the chin since the 1920's. To punch an opponent on the button is to punch him in a very vulnerable spot—just the right spot, so to speak. The term was being transferred to other kinds of accuracy by the mid-20th century, as in "On the button, a program ending exactly on time" (*Printer's Ink Monthly*, 1937).

on the fly
In passing, hurriedly, without pausing. The term comes from baseball's fly ball, a ball that is batted high into the air and, if caught before it bounces, counts as an out for the batter. From this came "catching a ball on the fly" (before it bounces), a term dating from the mid-19th century, which was later transferred to other hurried enterprises, as in "I only saw Mary on the fly, and barely had time to say hello."

on the nose
Accurately, precisely. This term seems to come from boxing, much like its close relative, ON THE BUTTON, and certainly a punch on the nose is a telling blow. In racing, however, a bet on the nose means a bet to win (that is, come in first), and in Australian slang, "on the nose" means offensive and smelly. In America, however, it has been used to signify exactitude and precision since the 1930's, as in "That is the right answer, sir. You've hit it right on the nose."

on the ropes
Helpless; close to ruin or failure. This term comes from boxing, where it alludes to the boxer who is stunned and hurt and therefore leans helplessly against the ropes of the ring. It has been used figuratively since the mid-20th century.

"My body could stand the crutches, but my mind couldn't stand the sidelines."

—MICHAEL JORDAN, injured Chicago Bulls basketball player, quoted in *Newsweek*, Jan. 5, 1987

on the sidelines

Out of the action; a spectator rather than a participant. This term refers to the area next to either sideline of a football field, where one is off the field itself. It also gave rise to the verb *to sideline*, meaning to prevent or remove someone from active participation. Both terms have been used figuratively since about 1930.

on track

On course, in the right direction. This particular Americanism seems to come from one or another kind of racing in which the competitors follow a track. (In contrast, a similar but older term, *off the track*, meaning "off course," probably comes from railroading, where it means derailed.) The current expression originated in the 20th century and began to be used figuratively only in the 1970's or so, as in "Mondale won the Illinois primary and said his comeback was on track" (*Gainesville Sun*, Apr. 3, 1984, cited by *OED*).

on your mark

A signal to begin. It comes from the starter's command to runners to assume a starting position in the starting blocks or on a starting platform, and often is followed by "Get set, Go!" It is occasionally transferred to beginning any enterprise.

open season on

A time when a person, object, idea, etc., is open to criticism or attack. The term comes from hunting and fishing, where it refers to a specific season or time of year when it is legal to fish or hunt for certain species that are protected at other times. It dates from the late 19th century and was being used figuratively by the early 20th century. For example, a *New York Times* headline for an article about a crackdown on evaders of subway fare-paying had it, "Open Season on Fare Beaters" (May 17, 1992). Oddly enough, the related term, *closed season*, the time of protection, is only rarely transferred to other enterprises.

outclass, to

To surpass by a wide margin; to be or appear to be far superior. This term was first used in several sports during the 19th century but may have originated in yachting, where "class" refers to a specific kind of boat. In racing of any kind it describes a competitor who is so far superior to the others that he/it seems to be in an altogether different (higher) class. It was being transferred to other undertakings by the late 19th century. For example, Arthur Quiller Couch had it in *Delectable Duchy* (1893): "As a liar I outclassed every other man on board." See also OUTDISTANCE.

outdistance, to

To defeat by a wide margin. The term comes from track and other kinds of racing, and refers to leaving the other competitors far behind. It dates from the mid-19th century and was being used figuratively by the end of the century, as in "The valedictorian had outdistanced the other students by at least ten grade points."

> "Sometimes he [Olivier Messiaen] would say things right out of left field that were wonderful. He told me I would benefit from studying rocks, that the different colors of rocks could tell me something about harmony."
>
> —Composer HERMAN WEISS, quoted by Richard Dyer, *Boston Globe*, May 8, 1992

out in left field, (way)

Out of touch, eccentric, odd; also, misguided. This term alludes to the left field of baseball, and there is some disagreement concerning its origin. Some writers suggest it comes from the remoteness of left field, but only in very asymmetrical ballparks is left field more distant than right field. Others suggest it alludes to the "wrongness" of left as opposed to the "rightness" of right. A correspondent of William Safire's in the *New York Times* said it was an insulting remark made to those who bought left-field seats in New York's Yankee Stadium during the years that Babe Ruth played right field, putting them far away from this outstanding player. Perhaps the most likely theory is that it alludes to inmates of the Neuropsychiatric Institute, a mental hospital, which was located behind left field in Chicago's old West Side Park. Hence being told you are "out in left field" would mean you were accused of being as peculiar as a mental patient. In any event, the term has been used figuratively for various kinds of eccentricity and misguidedness since the first half of the 20th century.

John Ciardi also cited a synonym, *out in left pickle*, maintaining that "pickle" was baseball slang for the outfield. Perhaps it once was, but it is no longer current.

out of bounds

Unfair, prohibited, forbidden. The bounds in this expression allude to the boundaries of the playing area in numerous sports, and by extension the rules that apply to them. In football, out of bounds means out of the playing area. A ball that is out of bounds is considered out of play but remains in the possession of the offensive team. In basketball, if either a player or a ball goes out of bounds, the ball goes to the opposing team. In soccer a ball that is out of bounds is put back in play by a throw-in made by a member of the opposing team. In golf out of bounds refers to the ground on which play is prohibited, which is marked by a fence, line, stakes, or some other means. When a golf ball is hit out of bounds, the stroke must be replayed from as near as possible to the point of the original stroke, and a penalty stroke is added to the player's score.

The term has been around since the early 19th century and began to be transferred to other kinds of prohibition by the 1940's. Football player Jim Brown used *Out of Bounds* as the title of his highly critical book (1989), in which he accused the NFL of racism.

out of one's league: *see* IN THE SAME LEAGUE.

> "*He doesn't count, does he? He is out of the running.*"
> —W. E. NORRIS, *Adrian Vidal* (1885)

out of the running
Not competing; having no chance of success. The term comes from horse racing, where a horse that has been scratched is termed out of the running. It was being transferred to more general kinds of elimination by the mid-19th century.

P P P P P

pacesetter: *see* SET THE PACE.

> *"With [Captain] Ray Bourque sitting in the press box,
> and their playoff dreams ready to book a first-class,
> one-way seat to Palookaville, the Bruins came out
> shoveling, bashing, bruising and otherwise kicking Ca-
> nadian kiesters up and down Causeway ice."*
> —KEVIN PAUL DUPONT, *Boston Globe,* May 8, 1992

palooka

An incompetent, inept person; a loser. This term was originally coined for an incompetent boxer by baseball player and
vaudeville performer Jack Conway (1886–1928), writing in *Variety.* Jack Dempsey defined it, "Anyone ... so inexperienced
or stupid that he can be hit by a swing is a palooka who can
be murdered by straight punches, hooks, or uppercuts."
Dating from the 1920's, it was soon applied to other loutish
athletes and then extended to any kind of incompetence.

paper chase

The pursuit of a college degree, diploma, or professional cer-
tificate, which generally involves a good deal of paperwork.
This term actually was the name of a race popular in English
schools during the 18th century, a version of what today is
called *hare and hounds.* Two runners carrying bags full of paper scraps would scatter handfuls at intervals, and other runners, starting behind them, would try to follow this paper trail
for five to ten miles or so. By the first half of the 20th century
the expression was being used figuratively for any enterprise
involving a good deal of paper. In America the expression's

currency was abetted by a motion picture, *The Paper Chase* (1973), a comedy-drama about the pressures of freshman year at Harvard Law School. It starred John Houseman as a tyrannical law professor, a role for which he won an Oscar and in which he continued in a subsequent television series based on the film.

par for the course

An average or normal amount; just what one might expect. The term comes from golf, where par for the course is the average number of strokes needed by an expert golfer to complete the entire course. Actually, it represents the theoretical standard for perfect play. The term began to be used figuratively for other kinds of expectation in the second half of the 20th century, as in "I missed three of the questions on the exam, which is par for the course."

"Too angry to parry, as she usually did, with wit."
—MARIA EDGEWORTH, *Patronage* (1814)

parry, to

To turn aside; to evade or dodge. The term comes from fencing, where since the 17th century or so it has meant a defensive action in which the fencer deflects the attacker's blade with his or her own blade. It was being used figuratively by the early 18th century.

penthouse

An apartment on the top floor or roof of a building, in the latter case usually set back from the outer walls. This term dates back as far as the 14th century, when it signified a shed or other subsidiary structure with a sloping roof. In the 17th century, however, it acquired another, sports-related meaning which persists. In court tennis the penthouse is the corridor with a sloping roof above the edges of the three "battery" walls, which the server must hit. It is presumably this sense that accounts for the modern meaning of a lofty dwelling.

"Let's get through these holidays without any more mess. . . . I don't want to give you a pep talk."
—JOHN O'HARA, *Appointment in Samarra* (1935)

pep talk

A vigorous speech intended to arouse enthusiasm and determination to succeed in an individual or group. The term dates from the 1920's and originally was used for the coach's traditional talk to a team before a game. (The word *pep* itself, dating from the mid-19th century and meaning "spirited vigor," is a shortening of "pepper" and alludes to that condiment's spiciness.) By the mid-20th century the expression had been transferred to talks given by business executives to their employees and the like. The related practice of holding a *pep rally*, where student enthusiasm was roused by means of songs, cheers, a march across campus, etc., also dates from about 1920 and was similarly transferred, although less frequently.

"Squash racquets is above all a percentage game."
—JACK BARNABY, *Winning Squash Racquets* (1979)

percentage play, a

A technique or strategy that has a good chance of success; a low-risk move. Although the idea long preceded it and the word "percentage" alone was used in a similar sense from the mid-19th century, the precise phrase here comes from baseball, where it began to be used in the 1930's. It designated a conservative play that, based on the law of averages, was likely to succeed, as opposed to an unusual or gambling play. Examples include a pitcher deliberately walking a strong batter, or a base runner waiting for a hit to advance rather than trying to steal a base. It was soon applied to similar strategy in other sports, such as tennis, and then used figuratively in other enterprises, as in "She was apt to try the discount store first, rather than hoping for a sale at the high-priced department store—a percentage play."

" 'Phantom' Is a Phenom; Advance Sales Beat 'Les Miz' Record"
—Headline, *Boston Globe*, May 23, 1992

phenom
A brilliant beginner; a fast starter. This word was coined about 1890 by sportswriters to describe a highly touted rookie. At first used in baseball, this abbreviation for "phenomenal player" soon was applied to boxers and other fine athletes. It continues to be so used but also has been transferred to star neophytes in any field of endeavor. Bud Collins had it in writing about the burnout of sixteen-year-old Jennifer Capriati, defeated in the third round of the 1992 Italian Open by a player ranked 25 places below her: "Her injury ... is old stuff for young phenoms: charred brain" (*Boston Globe*, May 8, 1992). And in the headline quoted above, concerning advance sales of the musical *Phantom of the Opera* beating the box-office record set by *Les Miserables* five years earlier, the term figures as a synonym for a fast start.

photofinish
An extremely close finish. The term originated in racing and refers to a finish so close that officials must examine a photograph of the conclusion to determine the winner. Photographing a race, and, simultaneously, recording the elapsed time, was first proposed by Gustavus T. Kirby, president emeritus of the U.S. Olympic Committee, about 1926. The same idea had occurred to C. H. Fetter, an electronics engineer, and together they perfected, a few years later, the Kirby Two-Eyed Camera. It was official for judging the 1932 Olympics at Los Angeles and for timing the decathlon. The Kirby used an electric clock. Four years later a somewhat different method, the photoelectric eye, began to be used at Florida's Hialeah racetrack. By 1940 the term had been transferred to other close races, as in the *Baltimore Sun*: "Gov. Payne H. Ratner ... emerged a photo-finish leader tonight in the complete unofficial count of ballots" (Nov. 22, 1940).

pinch hitter

A substitute. The term comes from baseball and was supposedly coined by sportswriter Charlie Dryden in 1892, when the practice of allowing a player to substitute for another at bat was first permitted. It refers to the fact that such a substitution was always made at a critical point or in a tight situation, which has been called a "pinch" since about 1489. The pinch hitter bats only once and the player he replaces is then removed from the game. When that player also is replaced in the field, the pinch hitter also is out of the game unless he takes a position in the field, in which case he becomes a *substitute*. One of the first batters to become famous as a pinch hitter was Johnny Doyle of the Cleveland Spiders. By the 1920's the term was being transferred to just about any kind of substitution, frequently but not always in some kind of emergency.

ping-pong, to

To bounce something—an object, an idea, a person, words— back and forth, more or less at random. The term comes from a game of table tennis played with wooden paddles and a celluloid ball manufactured in the late 19th century by J. Jacques and Son, who probably coined the name Ping-Pong for it (it is a trademark for table tennis in the United States). By about 1900 the verb form was being used figuratively for various kinds of back-and-forth exchange, especially batting around an idea without reaching a firm decision.

The game of ping-pong became especially popular in China, which has fielded numerous world champions. In 1971, after years of hostility, the first step toward resuming diplomatic relations between the United States and the mainland People's Republic of China was taken when the latter invited a U.S. table-tennis team to compete there. This step was dubbed *ping-pong diplomacy* by a journalist, a term immediately picked up by other writers.

pitch for, to

To work for a cause, organization, etc. The term comes from baseball, where it simply means to play for a team in the capacity of pitcher. By the 1940's it was being used figuratively to mean working for something else, as in "Johnson stayed in there, ready to pitch for the party when he was called from the bench" (*Time*, Mar. 14, 1949).

Since about the second half of the 19th century pitching a ball has also been transferred to uttering words, on both sides of the Atlantic. (What is now called "bowling" to the batsman in cricket used to be called "pitching," as of course it still is in baseball.) Thus we have the old-fashioned American slang expression *pitching woo*, for courtship, and the modern *sales pitch*; both are forms of throwing words, as it were, to promote a particular view. Similarly related are the *pitchman*, originally a hawker of street wares and now usually simply an advertiser, and the verb form, *to make a pitch* for something or someone.

pit stop
A brief stop to rest, eat, use a bathroom, etc. The term comes from automobile racing, where it refers to a driver stopping the automobile during a race in a pit, an area near the track, where the car can be refueled, receive new tires, or be otherwise repaired. (The pit was originally so called, from the 1930's on, because it was an excavation a number of feet lower than the car, enabling mechanics to get underneath the engine for repairs.)

In speedway races the pits are usually located on a road parallel to the main straightaway. In drag racing pits are usually parking lots. At one of the oldest (run since 1911) and perhaps most famous auto race, the Indianapolis 500, an effective pit stop in 1992—to pump forty gallons of fuel, change four wheels, and make any minor adjustments—took approximately fifteen seconds.

The term began to be used figuratively for other kinds of brief stop in the second half of the 20th century.

Play ball!
Begin; get started. This imperative is the traditional baseball umpire's call to begin a game (or re-start after time out, as for a rain delay), and it dates back at least as far as 1867. It occasionally is transferred to other kinds of beginning. Its association with base-

ball was chronicled by Ogden Nash in a poem published by *Sports Illustrated* in 1957: "All winter long ... The sports pages are strictly no soap, And until the cry of Play Ball! I simply mope."

play ball with, to
To cooperate, to get along with. It is not clear exactly which sport this term comes from. In colloquial American speech, playing ball with someone may refer to a game of baseball or basketball. However, the term was first used figuratively in England, so more likely cricket or rounders or rugby was the original source. Hugh McHugh had it in *Back to the Woods* (1903): "Well, if Bunch should refuse to play ball I could send the check back to Uncle Peter" (cited by *OED*).

> "Asking him to be an impartial play-by-play announcer would be no different from sending Captain Ahab after bay scallops."
> —Sportswriter VIC ZEIGEL on Phil Rizzuto's partisan style

play-by-play
A detailed verbal account of some action or activity. The term comes from sportscasting in the early 1920's and may have been coined by Red Barber, for years the voice of the Brooklyn Dodgers. Radio broadcasts of games must be fairly detailed descriptions of what is happening, since the radio audience, unlike television viewers, cannot see anything that is occurring. The first radio broadcast featuring such a running description took place in 1921, over Pittsburgh station KDKA, of a game between the Pirates and the Phillies. The first major telecast took place in 1939, with Red Barber describing a game between the Dodgers and the Cincinnati Reds. See also the somewhat newer term BLOW-BY-BLOW.

play catch-up: *see* CATCH-UP.

player
Active participant. This term is a very broad one, being used for virtually every participant in any team sport. In the late

20th century it began to be adopted in both business and politics. The term has been used, William Safire's correspondents report, for individuals bidding for a company and for persons involved in Washington political stories. It also is used for organizations, as in "The television service that brings viewers up-to-the-minute market information has itself become an important player in the stock market."

A further emphasis on importance is provided by *major player*, meaning a key participant. Presumably a shortening of "major-league player," it, too, is applied to individuals ("Mulroney is no longer a major player in Canadian politics") and to organizations ("Its latest exhibit is making this small gallery a major player on the art scene").

play fair, to
To play in accordance with the rules; to avoid cheating; to behave honorably. This term is very old indeed, first appearing in a York mystery play of about 1440: "Playes faire in feere [fear]." It means practically the same thing as FAIR PLAY and has long been similarly transferred.

"I'm throwing the ball twice as hard as I ever did. The ball's just not getting there as fast."

—LEFTY GOMEZ, New York Yankees pitcher

play hardball, to

To hold nothing back; to behave aggressively and ruthlessly. The term comes from baseball, which uses a so-called hardball, smaller but actually only a little harder than a softball. The baseball usage dates from the early 19th century, and became a metaphor for ruthless behavior only in the 1970's. Thus a *Boston Globe* obituary of Lee Atwater, chairman of the Republican National Committee, said, "He relished the role of a hardball player in national politics" (Mar. 30, 1991). In a notorious incident in Los Angeles in which four policemen were videotaped while beating a suspect, Rodney King, one of them was quoted as jeering their victim in the hospital with "We played a little hardball tonight, and you lost" (*Time*, Apr. 8, 1991). From its innocuous meaning in the sport, "hardball" has been changed into one with sinister implications.

playing against air

In a precarious position. The term comes from football, where it refers to playing without the customary opposition of another player. For example, a linebacker usually has an opposing tight end lined up on his side, but for one reason or another the opponent is sometimes absent. The term has been occasionally used figuratively in the late 20th century.

> *"As Duke Ellington once said, the Battle of Waterloo was won on the playing fields of Elkton."*
> —BABE RUTH, attributed by Grantland Rice,
> *The Tumult and the Shouting* (1954)

playing fields of Eton, the

School sports provide the training needed for success on the battlefield. The term is from a famous remark long attributed to the Duke of Wellington, who supposedly made it while watching a cricket match at the famous English public school of Eton a decade after Napoleon's decisive feat at Waterloo (June 18, 1815). Its complete form, supposedly bowdlerized by Babe Ruth in the quotation above, is "The Battle of Waterloo was won on the playing fields of Eton." Both the Duke and his family denied his ever having uttered these words, but they still are attributed to him and used as a symbol of certain upper-class British values. Moreover, the sentiment persists as well in such statements as "The sports of the people afford an index to the character of the nation" (Frederick W. Hackwood, *Old English Sports*, 1907).

playing games

Also, *to play games*. Toying with someone over a serious matter; behaving evasively or deceitfully. It is not certain whether this term originally alluded to cheating at cards or in a sport, but it is old enough to have long been proverbial. It is sometimes put as *playing at some game*, as in Edward Fitzgerald's letter of June 12, 1845: "I ... told him two could play at that game." See also HOW YOU PLAY THE GAME; PLAY THE GAME.

playoff
An extension of a contest to determine the winner when both sides are tied. The term comes from sports, where it has two meanings: (1) a single game or series of games to determine the winner when there is a tie; (2) a series of previously scheduled post-season sports contests played among the top teams of their leagues in baseball, basketball, football, and ice hockey, to name just a few. An example of the latter is the League Championship Series played every year between the first teams in the Eastern and Western divisions of each major baseball league.

Among the most dramatic tie-breaking playoffs in baseball history was the game at Ebbets Field between the New York Giants and Brooklyn Dodgers at the end of the 1951 season, for the National League Championship. The Giants won thanks to Bobby Thomson's home run but then lost the World Series to the New York Yankees (also see under NINTH-INNING RALLY). Another example was the game played by the New York Yankees against the Boston Red Sox at Fenway Park in October, 1976. The winning run was a late-inning homer by light-hitting shortstop Bucky Dent, with Red Sox slugger Carl Yastremski popping up for the final out.

> *"If a Ball be stop'd by any person, Horse, Dog, or anything else, the Ball so stopped must be played where it lies."*
>
> —St. Andrews Code (1754)

play the ball as/where it lies
Make the best of whatever circumstances exist. This has been the golden rule in golf ever since it was first set forth in the famous St. Andrews Code. In the 20th century it has occasionally been transferred to other circumstances. After contracting a rare disease, champion golfer Bobby Jones told reporters, "It's going to get worse all the time, but don't fret. Remember, we 'play the ball where it lies,' and now let's not talk about this ever again."

play the field, to
To avoid committing oneself to a single course of action; also, to date or court more than one person at a time. This term comes from 19th-century British horse racing, where it meant to bet on every horse running in a race in hopes of winning a LONG SHOT that would yield a huge profit. It was transferred to other enterprises in the 20th century.

> "The voice of the schoolboy rallies the ranks: 'Play up! play up! and play the game!' "
> —HENRY JOHN NEWBOLT (1862–1938), *Vitai Lampada*

play the game, to
To behave fairly and honorably; to obey the rules. This term alludes to fair play in sports, and has done so since ancient Greek times. Michael Gorra used it as the title of a 1991 novel about the Indian cricketer K. S. Ranjitsinhji, who at the turn of the 20th century was the greatest cricketer of his time, the star of England's national team, and who, when he put his bat aside, stepped onto the throne of the princely state of Nawanagar. The title alludes to the lesson he learned early at a school run by the British Raj for Indian princes, that cricket provided a metaphor for a gentlemanly code of conduct. It is this sense that survives in the figurative use of the expression. See also HOW YOU PLAY THE GAME; PLAYING GAMES.

> "I scorn to poach for power."
> —JOHN DRYDEN and N. LEE, *The Duke of Guise*, 4:3 (1682)

poach, to
To encroach on someone else's property, rights, ideas, or the like. This word began to be used about 1600 for the illegal taking of game and fish and was being used figuratively by the end of the 17th century. It also acquired specific significance in several sports. In tennis, squash, handball, and similar ball games, it has been used, since the late 19th century, for entering a partner's section of the court or field and playing the ball he or she would normally have played. In tennis (dou-

bles), poaching at the net is an especially effective offensive tactic. In horse racing, crew, and other kinds of race, poaching means to take an unfair advantage at the start, by starting either early or some distance ahead of the other competitors; this usage, too, dates from the late 19th century, but is more common in Great Britain than America.

pole position: *see under* INSIDE TRACK

> "*Dressing a pool player in a tuxedo is like putting whipped cream on a hot dog.*"
> —MINNESOTA FATS, *Sports Illustrated*, Apr. 4, 1966

poolroom (atmosphere)
Describing a shady, somewhat sleazy place inhabited by drifters, bookies, and other individuals of dubious character. This Americanism derives from the character and reputation of the 19th-century establishments where pool and billiards were played and illegal betting was carried on. Indeed, the word "poolroom" itself became synonymous with bookmaking. In the 20th century the term began to be transferred to other dubious places and enterprises. Today the old connotations persist, even though many if not most modern American poolrooms are perfectly respectable establishments and attract quite legitimate customers.

> "*Serious sport has nothing to do with fair play. It is bound up with hatred, jealousy, boastfulness, disregard of all rules, and sadistic pleasure in witnessing violence: in other words, it is war minus the shooting.*"
> —GEORGE ORWELL, *Shooting an Elephant* (1950)

poor sport/sore loser
A person who is peevish, resentful, and/or rude in defeat; one who exhibits some or all of the characteristics described in the quotation above. To these one could add readiness to take unfair advantage whenever possible, discourtesy toward opponents, and gracelessly crowing and bragging in victory. Both expressions, which represent the antithesis of the GOOD

LOSER/SPORT, appear to be American in origin but are now used on both sides of the Atlantic. See also SPORTSMANSHIP.

pop-up
Describing an object in which a component or other object is caused to burst upward suddenly. Such objects include *pop-up books*, in which three-dimensional pieces of artwork are raised from the pages when they are opened; *pop-up toasters*, which eject toasted bread slices when they are finished; cameras with *pop-up flash* mechanisms, which are activated when light conditions call for them; etc. The earliest use of the word "pop-up" was in mid-19th-century baseball, where it denoted, as it still does, a high, short fly ball that can be easily caught (it is also called a *pop fly*). It seems reasonable to suppose that this usage was transferred to other pop-up devices, beginning in the first half of the 20th century.

power hitter
An individual who can be counted on to perform well, especially when needed. The term comes from baseball, where it denotes a batter noted for hitting home runs. It began to be used figuratively, particularly in American politics, in the second half of the 20th century, as in "When it comes to campaign fund-raising, Jones is a power hitter."

> *"The Church was making a last desperate power play."*
> —*New York Review of Books* (1976)

power play
An aggressive action or strategy that marshals one's strength in order to overcome opposition or win control. The term is used in a number of sports, but probably was used first in American football, where it denotes a running play in which the offensive blockers converge and run ahead of the ball-carrier in order to clear his way. In ice hockey and soccer the term means that one team temporarily has more men on the ice or the field than the other (because one or more of the opposing team are in the penalty box); they therefore are able to

mount a concerted attack on the opponent's goal. The term began to be used figuratively from about 1965 on. L. Mosley had it as the title of a 1973 book, *Power Play: The Tumultuous World of Mideast Oil.*

pro

Expert. This abbreviation for "professional," as distinct from "amateur," was being used in sports by the end of the 18th century. The designation at first signified a class distinction, the professional being one who earned a living from a sport whereas the amateur was a gentleman who participated only for pleasure. In the 19th century the professional athlete who participated for financial gain was barred from amateur-level competition, including the Olympic Games (which were revived in the late 19th century). Today these distinctions are ignored in some sports but retained in somewhat different form in others (college versus pro football, for example). In modern athletic terminology the word *pro* is used both adjectivally, as in the preceding sentence, and as a noun, where it most often designates an expert hired to instruct members and run the *pro shop* at a club or resort. Figuratively, it has been used loosely for any kind of expert since about 1900. C. J. Cutliffe Hyne had it in *Mr. Horrocks, Purser* (1902): " 'I tell you the man's not a theatrical [actor]' ... 'Never knew any pro yet bring either honour or profit to any boat,' said the Purser" (cited by *OED*).

> *"It's not that I'm psyched out by him, but I'm playing great and he hits three all-time winners."*
> —Tennis article, *The New Yorker*, Aug. 10, 1978

psych(ed) out, to (be)

To intimidate someone; to lose one's nerve. This particular usage appears to have originated in skiing, where, since the 1960's, it has meant to lose one's courage on a downhill course. It was quickly taken up in surfing, where it alluded to a surfer's fear when encountering a big wave. It has been used for all kinds of similar situations from about 1970 on. Alone or with the word "up" replacing "out," it took on a slightly different meaning as well, *to be psyched (up)* meaning to be psychologically prepared to do one's best in some situation (for example, "I'm really psyched up for this interview").

> *"And they [the authors] pull no punches in accusing General Schwarzkopf of complicity in deceiving the public on the magnitude of Iraqi casualties."*
> —JAMES BLACKWELL, *New York Times*, Sept. 5, 1991

pull no punches, to
To behave without restraint; to hold nothing back. The term comes from boxing, where to pull a punch means to hit with less than full force. It began to be used figuratively in the first half of the 20th century. Sportswriter Dick Schaap had it: "You say something [derogatory] in print about a guy [Yogi Berra] and he says, 'Hi! How you doing?' the next time you see him.... It doesn't make you wish you had pulled your punch, but it does make you think what a remarkable guy you have covered."

pull one's own weight, to
To do one's share; to take responsibility for oneself. The term comes from rowing, where a crew member must pull on an

oar hard enough to propel his or her own weight. In use literally since the mid-19th century, it began to be used figuratively in the 1890's.

> *"If you ever get belted and see three fighters through a haze, go after the one in the middle. That's what ruined me—I went after the two guys on the end."*
> —MAX BAER, heavyweight champion (1934–35)

punch drunk
Also, *punchy*. Dazed, confused. The term comes from boxing, where it signifies the long-term effect of repeated blows to the head. Frequently causing repeated concussion, they result in unsteady gait, blurred vision, slowed-down movements and speech, and generally dulled mental functioning. The term dates from about 1910 and began to be used figuratively by the 1920's.

> *"I . . . woke at seven feeling like Henry Cooper's punchbag."*
> —DICK FRANCIS, *Slay-Ride* (1973)

punching bag
A victim or scapegoat; an object of abuse. The term alludes to the inflated or stuffed bag used in training boxers. Generally suspended at an appropriate height, it enables fighters to practice different kinds of punch and the footwork associated with them. The term dates from the late 19th century and began to be used figuratively in the second half of the 20th century.

punch line
The words expressing the ultimate point of a joke or story. The term alludes to the boxer's punch, or blow, and has been used figuratively since about 1920, as in "All of their sure-fire punch-lines went over" (*Variety*, Nov. 25, 1921; cited by *OED*).

push comes to shove, if/when
If worst comes to worst; in the most serious circumstances.
This term appears to come from rugby, a game better known
in Britain than in America. It is played by two teams of fifteen players with an inflated oval ball on a large rectangular
field. For common infractions of the rules, a *scrum* (similar to
a face-off) is formed at the point of infraction. Eight forwards
from each team take part, and they push against one another
until one of their teammates can kick the ball back out of the
scrum to the backs to start the team's offense. When this push
comes to (i.e., becomes) shove, the game is resumed. The term
has been used figuratively, on both sides of the Atlantic, since
the mid-20th century.

put one's oar in, to
To contribute one's opinion or otherwise interfere in someone
else's affairs. The term refers to giving one's presumably un-
wanted help in rowing a boat and dates from about 1700. It
was being used figuratively by the 1730's and remains current.

put on the gloves, to
To be ready to fight. The gloves alluded to are boxing gloves,
which were routinely used only from the 1870's on. The figurative expression dates from the early 20th century, as in
"Furious at this new turn of events in the office, Harry was
all set to put on the gloves."

put up your dukes
Prepare to fight. The word "dukes" has been British slang for
the hands or fists since the second half of the 19th century.
Hotten's 1874 compendium of slang defines the term as "a
kind invitation to fight," but whether it originated among
prizefighters or in less formal bouts is not certain. In any
event, the term crossed the Atlantic and made its way into
novels featuring lowbrow slang.

"You and me couldn't put enough together between us to pick up a couple of cooled pieces. And who'd do the quarterbackin'?"

—TOM KAKONIS, *Crisscross* (1990)

quarterback, to

To direct or guide. The quarterback's role in football is, of course, one of leadership. Stationed directly behind the center, he calls the signals to begin a play, receives the ball when it is snapped back, and on most plays passes it to a receiver or hands off to a running back. As John Madden put it, "When the game starts, a quarterback must be a leader, a field general" (*Hey, Wait a Minute*, 1984). And former Notre Dame football coach Ara Parseghian said, "Every successful coach must have a successful quarterback" (*Sports Illustrated*, Apr. 24, 1967).

The name "quarterback" for this player dates from the 1870's and originally alluded to his lining up approximately a quarter of the way into the backfield (halfbacks and fullbacks take positions farther behind the line of scrimmage). In the 20th century it was occasionally transferred to the player in other sports, such as basketball, who is primarily responsible for handling the ball and directing the team's offense. Its figurative use in verb form dates from about 1940.

rabbit punch
An unfair blow. The term comes from boxing, where it signifies an illegal clubbing blow to the back of the neck, usually
done with the back of the fist. It is judged a foul and is penalized with either the loss of points or disqualification. The term
dates from about 1910 and began to be transferred in the latter part of the 20th century.

racehorse
A brilliant achiever. Horses began to be bred for the sport of
racing—the so-called THOROUGHBRED—in the early 17th century, and the word "racehorse" dates from this period. Not
until the 20th century was the word used figuratively, both in
and out of sports. In basketball it is used adjectivally for an
aggressive style of play characterized by much running and
fast breaks, with little use of set plays or attention to defense.
In a more general sense it has been applied to, for example,
a brilliant student, as in "She was the racehorse of her high
school class, not only pulling a straight A average but taking
many college courses as well."

racing form
A complete tally of background information. In horse racing,
it designates a printed chart giving the past performances of
the horses entered in a race, the conditions of the race, the
probable odds, background data on the jockeys, and similar information. The term dates from the mid-20th century, and in
recent decades has been used figuratively for similar compila-
tions of information, as in "His new publication aspires to be
the racing form of the software industry."

rain check
A postponement of an invitation or sale offer; also, a ticket for
future use for a postponed event. The practice of giving rain

checks originated in the 1880's in baseball, which had been charging admission for games since 1858. In that year the Brooklyn and New York City "all-star" teams rented a Long Island racetrack for a "championship" series of three games, and charged 50 cents admission to the 1,500 spectators who showed up. The rain check was first offered, as it still is, to those who had paid admission for a game that was postponed or interrupted owing to bad weather or some similar unavoidable circumstance. The practice was formalized in the National League constitution of 1890, and the term was being transferred to other kinds of ticket by the early 20th century. By the mid-20th century it also was used for a coupon entitling a customer to purchase at a later date, and for the same price, a sale item that was temporarily out of stock. Finally, in underworld slang a rain check has meant a parole since about 1930.

rain out, to

To cause a postponement or cancellation. The term originated in various kinds of athletic event that must be postponed or canceled owing to rain (it is then termed a *rainout*). It has been used in sports since the early 20th century and was soon transferred to other events so affected by weather—picnics (see an example under CALL THE GAME), airplane flights, and so on.

razz, to

To tease or heckle. This term comes from the *raspberry* or *razzberry*, a somewhat older synonym of BRONX CHEER. However, it appears to have been used first for the treatment accorded boxers by a less than polite crowd, beginning about 1915. It subsequently was extended to mean any kind of teasing, both gentle and hostile, directed in private or in public.

real McCoy, the

The genuine article. This term is widely believed to come from the stage name Kid McCoy, taken by a very able young boxer named Norman Selby (1873–1914). For many years he

fought approximately once a month and won most of the
bouts by a knockout. In hopes of drawing larger crowds, other
boxers adopted the same name, but in 1899, Selby won a spectacular victory over Joe Choynski in the twentieth round,
which was reported in the next day's *San Francisco Examiner* under the headline "Now You've Seen the Real McCoy."
There are several other theories as to the term's origin, some
relating it to the brand name of a scotch whisky, but the boxing one is widely enough held to earn the term a place in this
book.

> *"Many a heart is caught in the rebound, i.e., after a
> repulse by another."*
>
> —VINCENT LEAN, *Collecteana* (1902)

rebound
Resilience; bounding back after a setback. This term has been
used for the return of a ball from a wall, goalpost, etc., after
an unsuccessful shot since the 16th century, when Palsgrave
defined it in his dictionary of 1530. Today it retains a specific
meaning in numerous sports. In ice hockey it describes a puck
that bounces off the goalkeeper, crossbar, goalpost, or boards
and remains in play, as well as a goal scored off it. In rugby
it is a ball that hits a player's body (other than the hand, arm,
or lower leg) and bounces forward but is not a knock-on and
may be played again by that same player. The most frequent
sports usage in America is in basketball, where a rebound is
the carom off the basket rim or backboard of a missed shot, as
well as the act of gaining control of such a ball. Scoring off
such shots is a highly desirable skill. In the 1991–92 college
season a small Massachusetts university, Fitchburg State, had
the unique distinction of boasting the nation's top rebounders
in both women's and men's basketball, a first in NCAA history. Malane Perry led the women with 17.7 rebounds a game,
and her seasonal total of 442 rebounds led all teams in all divisions, male and female. Jeff Black topped the men with 16.5
rebounds per game.
     The term was used figuratively for other kinds of bounc-

ing back from the late 16th century on. Today it often refers
to affairs of the heart, to be *on the rebound* signifying that
one is trying to recover from an unhappy love affair by
quickly engaging in another.

relay

A series of persons taking turns or shifts, or relieving one another. The earliest use of this term was in hunting, where it
meant getting fresh hounds for the chase. Later it signified a
fresh supply of horses obtained at various points along a jour-
ney, but in the late 19th century it again became more closely
associated with sports, particularly the various kinds of *relay
race* in track and swimming.

rhubarb

An argument or heated dispute. This Americanism was popularized by sportscaster Red Barber, who used it in a 1938 radio broadcast to describe a game-stopping fracas. Barber
claimed he got it from Garry Schumacher, who in turn ascribed it to New York sportswriter Tom Meany; Barber then
wrote about it in his *Rhubarb in the Catbird Seat* (1968). At
any rate, despite seeming illogic (how does this fruit resemble
a fight?) it quickly entered the vocabulary, first to describe
any fierce dispute on the field during a ball game, and later to
similar arguments anywhere.

ride, to

To annoy or tease someone. This American colloquialism appears to have originated in baseball, where it was used as
long ago as 1912 to describe heckling opponents or officials
during a game. It has nothing to do with transport but may
have been a shortening of "riding someone's back." The term
has slightly specialized meanings in other sports. In wrestling
it denotes maintaining control over one's opponent on the mat;
in lacrosse it means charging an opponent or using a pressing
defense against a particular opponent. But it is the baseball
usage that has been extended to mean general ridicule and
harassment.

ride the bench, to
To be regularly relegated to being a bystander rather than an active participant. The term comes from various American team sports—baseball, football, hockey, etc.—where it signifies spending most of one's time as a substitute rather than a regular team member. Also see under BENCH.

> "*I knew right off the bat.*"
> —F. W. BRONSON, *Nice People Don't Kill* (1940)

right off the bat
Instantly, immediately. This term alludes to the ball being hit off a baseball bat and has been used figuratively since the first half of the 20th century. The British locution *off one's own bat*, on the other hand, comes from cricket and means to manage without anyone else's help.

ringer
A superior substitute, brought in to strengthen a team, organization, or the like. This term comes from horse racing, where since the late 19th century it has meant the fraudulent entry in a race of a superior horse under another horse's name, so as to get better odds. It later was extended to similar frauds in other races (automobile, bicycle, etc.), as well as to more harmless kinds of substitute: for example, "The tenor section sounds much better now that we've hired some ringers from the opera company."

> "*Boxers need somewhere to fight, and that is why we have this square we call a ring.*"
> HENRY COOPER, *Henry Cooper's Book of Boxing* (1982)

ringside seat
A good vantage point. This term probably originated in 19th-century boxing, where it denoted the seats just outside the boxing ring. Despite its name, the ring is approximately twenty feet square (not round), and is raised on a platform three to four feet high. It is usually surrounded by three par-

allel ropes, at two-, three-, and four-foot heights, connected to a post at each corner by padded buckles. The ring floor consists of a layer of felt or rubber covered with taut canvas and extends about two feet beyond the ropes on all sides.

The term "ringside seat" dates as far back as the 1860's. During the course of the century, however, it began to be used quite generally for a good view (literal or figurative) of any event, not necessarily an athletic one. For example, "The Browns showed endless slides of their vacations, and for some reason we always had ringside seats."

riposte

An effective reply; a counterstroke. This term comes from fencing, where it signifies an offensive movement by a fencer after he or she has successfully parried an attack. It has been so used since about 1700, when this French word was adopted into English. It began to be used figuratively in the mid-19th century. The verb form, *to riposte*, meaning to make such a counterstroke (literally or figuratively), dates from the same periods.

> "*The rodeo cowboy represents the last frontier of the pure, unpampered athlete.*"
>
> —GORDON HANSEN, quoted by Robert
> Creamer, *Sports Illustrated*, Nov. 9, 1970

rodeo

A contest or competition. This word originally was simply Spanish for "roundup." With the decline of cattle-raising in the American West, however, it began to be used exclusively for a public exhibition of cowboy skills, including bronco riding, roping, and the like. By the 1920's it was being transferred to just about any kind of public competition—baby contests (for the prettiest baby), fishing (for the biggest fish caught), bicycle racing, etc. Soon it was being used even more loosely, as in "Nazi bombers smashed at London . . . in their fourth consecutive dusk-to-dawn rodeo of destruction" (*Baltimore Sun*, Sept. 11, 1940; cited by *OED*).

roll with the punches, to
To be resilient; to take adversity in stride. The term comes from boxing, where it means to move one's head and body in the same direction as the opponent's blow in order to diminish its effect. By the mid-20th century it was being used figuratively.

> *"Rooting for the New York Yankees is like rooting for U.S. Steel."*
>
> —Sportscaster RED SMITH, 1951

root for, to
To support vigorously; to cheer for. This Americanism originated in late 19th-century ballparks and signified the action of fans cheering loudly for their favorites. One writer suggests it comes from the old British dialect verb, *to rout*, meaning to shout. Another believes that it alludes to a fan's being "rooted" (attached) to the home team. The latter theory is supported by the lyrics to the unofficial baseball anthem, *Take Me Out to the Ball Game* (1908), "Root, root, root for the home team, If they don't win it's a shame." The earliest reference in print is dated 1897, but by the early 20th century the term was being used figuratively for any kind of strong support, verbal or simply moral. Smith's reference above is, of course, obsolete on two counts. Neither U.S. Steel nor the Yankees seem as invincible in the 1990's as they did in the 1950's (the team won the World Series in 1949–54, 1956, 1958, 1961–62).

> *"I had spent nearly a year [on the brig] and got the first rough and tumble of sea life."*
>
> —RICHARD DANA, *Two Years Before the Mast* (1840)

rough-and-tumble
Describing haphazard, unrestrained fighting or give-and-take. The term comes from boxing, where it has meant a fight without rules since the late 18th century (a practice eliminated from professional prizefighting when the Marquis of Queens-

berry Rules were adopted). "Biting or gouging, or worse practice, common in what is called rough-and-tumble," wrote H. H. Brackenridge in *Modern Chivalry* (1792). By the mid-19th century the term was being used figuratively.

In other sports the term *rough play*, used since the early 19th century for illegal body contact or unsportsmanlike roughness, usually incurs a penalty of some kind. Specifically, in football *unnecessary roughness*, *roughing the passer*, and *roughing the kicker* all incur a personal foul. In hockey there is a two-minute penalty for *roughing*, that is, an infraction too mild to incur the five-minute penalty for *fighting*. And in basketball, a *flagrant foul* is incurred for rough, unsportsmanlike conduct.

> *"When I first joined the Giants, I had what is known as the 'old roundhouse curve,' which is no more than a big, slow outdrop."*
>
> —CHRISTY MATHEWSON, *Pitching* (1912)

roundhouse

A vigorous blow. Although this term originally comes from the circular building with a revolving floor intended for the servicing and repair of railroad locomotives, that usage gave way to others in a variety of sports. The earliest and most familiar of these is the *roundhouse punch* of boxing, a hook delivered with a wide swing (alluding to the roundhouse's revolving floor). Much newer and less widely known is the *roundhouse kick* of karate, rendered by holding one leg out at the side of the body and bringing it forward in a wide horizontal arc while pivoting on the other foot. In baseball the term *roundhouse* has been used for a wide-sweeping curveball since about 1910. In figurative usage, however, it is the roundhouse punch that has been transferred to various literal and, sometimes, figurative blows.

rub of the green, the

Luck, fate. This term comes from golf, where since 1842 or so it has designated the accidental stoppage or deflection of a moving ball by an outside agency. For a much longer time, *the rub* has been used figuratively for a difficulty or obstruction to be overcome—Shakespeare had it in *Hamlet*: "To sleep; perchance to dream: aye, there's the rub" (3:1)—and this usage came from lawn bowls, where a rub is a bare or uneven patch of turf that deflects the bowl. The golf term was transferred to other kinds of impediment only in the first half of the 20th century and is more common in Britain than America.

rugby shirt

A long-sleeved knitted sports shirt featuring a pattern of bold horizontal stripes and a white collar and placket. An imitation of the shirts—in Britain called rugby jerseys—worn by rugby teams, it became a popular American collegiate style in the 1960's and 1970's, even though rugby itself is relatively un-

known in America (compared to football and soccer; see also
PUSH COMES TO SHOVE). The game, actually an ancestor of
American football, is named for Rugby School in England,
where it developed early in the 19th century. Supposedly it
grew out of an incident in which a soccer player, in a fit of
frustration, ran with the ball. On the school grounds to this
day there is a plaque that reads: "This stone commemorates
the exploit of William Webb Ellis, who, with a fine disregard
for the rules of football [i.e., called soccer in America] as
played in his time, first took the ball in his arms and ran with
it, thus originating the distinctive feature of the Rugby game,
A.D. 1823." This appears to be the only documentation concerning rugby's beginnings; the modern rules were developed
later. Rugby is popular as both an amateur and a professional
sport in Britain, Australia, New Zealand, France, and some
other countries. There is a league in the United States, but
the sport has not won nearly as much popularity here as the
rugby shirt.

run but can't hide, he/you can
Evasion won't avert a defeat. This expression was first attributed to heavyweight champion Joe Louis, who after defeating
the quick-moving Billy Conn by a knockout on June 19, 1946,
said, "He can run but he can't hide." President Ronald
Reagan alluded to it in 1985, warning terrorists, "You can run
but you can't hide." It came up again in a television newscast
in April, 1992, about Massachusetts instituting the use of
"wanted" posters, complete with their photographs, for di-
vorced fathers delinquent in making court-ordered child-
support payments. "They can run but they can't hide," the
newscasters said.

run for one's money, to have/give (someone) a
A close contest. This term probably comes from horse racing.
The "have" version presumably alludes to deriving pleasure
from an exciting race even if one does not win one's bets, the
satisfaction thus constituting payment. It first appeared in a
slang dictionary of 1874. The "give" version signifies present-

ing someone with a challenge in the form of a close contest.
Both versions were being used figuratively by the late 19th
century.

run interference, to
To handle troublesome problems or otherwise clear the way
for another person. The term comes from football, where it
designates both legitimate and illegal plays. Offensive interference signifies the act of an offensive player running ahead
of the receiver to block out defensive players. Such blocking
can be performed legally to create a hole for the receiver.
However, if a defensive player pushes or gets in the way of an
offensive receiver who is trying to catch a forward pass *before*
he makes the catch, he is guilty of defensive pass interference,
which is illegal.

The football term began to be used figuratively about
the mid-20th century, as in "John was excellent at running
interference for his boss, dealing with numerous time-
consuming problems and allowing her to focus on overall
strategy."

runner's knee
Various knee injuries triggered by running, but especially
chondromalacia and other injuries to the kneecap. They include loose cartilage, strained tendons and muscle attach-
ments, and inflamed nerves. From the 1960's on, as running
became an increasingly popular form of exercise among otherwise nonathletic individuals, the incidence of such injuries
increased exponentially. See also FOOTBALL KNEE.

"No man would run for president with a woman run
ning mate."
—*Daily Oklahoman*, Sept. 21, 1947

running mate
A fellow candidate for a lesser office linked with a more important one; specifically, the candidate for vice-president of
the United States. This Americanism probably comes from

horse racing, where it denotes a horse entered in a race in order to set the pace for another horse from the same stable,
which is expected to win. Although the connection does not
seem to be verifiable, the usage of "running" in the sense of
standing for office, and its connection with racing, can be seen
in this 1830 article from a Maine paper, the *Wiscasset Citizen*:
"Such politicians . . . bet on a candidate's running for the Chief
Magistracy of the Union or of a single State, precisely as they
would bet on the running of a race horse."

Dating from about 1860, the expression was being transferred to political candidates by 1900, and in that year was
used for William McKinley's running mate in the presidential
election.

running start
A head start; an initial advantage. The term comes from various kinds of racing in which a contestant is already in motion
before reaching the official starting point. In automobile racing the competing cars are already moving as they cross the
starting line or receive the starting signal. In track events
such as the running broad jump, the contestant normally
takes a hop, step, and jump in order to get momentum. This
term, which dates from about 1920, was being used figuratively by mid-century, as in "His extensive experience with
automobile production gave him a running start on the competition." Also see FLYING START.

run-off
An additional decisive election to determine which of the candidates actually wins. The term comes from racing, where it
denotes a final deciding race after a DEAD HEAT. About 1920 it
began to be transferred to elections, mainly in America and
principally to primaries, to decide which of the two leading
candidates of the primary garners the largest number of
votes.

run out the clock, to

Also, *kill the clock*. To use various delaying tactics to gain some advantage. The term comes from a number of sports—basketball, football, ice hockey, field hockey—in which playing time is specifically set. It refers to any strategy to protect one's lead by using up the remaining time, most often by keeping possession of the ball or puck so that the opposing team has no chance to score. In the second half of the 20th century it began to be used figuratively for similar deliberate procrastination in other endeavors, as in "We want to run out the clock on the strike deadline."

> *"The unspeakable in full pursuit of the uneatable, as Oscar Wilde described the class-ridden English sport of fox hunting, ran to ground a bill to ban the sport today."*
> —CRAIG WHITNEY, *New York Times*, Feb. 15, 1992

run to ground, to

To track to the absolute limit; to destroy. The term comes from fox hunting, where it denotes chasing the fox back to its burrow. The literal expression dates from the late 18th century, and it was used figuratively by the 1870's. It is sometimes put as *run into the ground*, as in "Those religionists ... are running religion, and morals, and progress into the ground" (Mrs. Stone, *My Wife and I*, 1871).

> *"Running with the ball is only one of three factors I use in rating a running back. The other two are pass-receiving and pass-blocking."*
> —JOHN MADDEN, *One Knee Equals Two Feet* (1986)

run with the ball, to

To make rapid progress toward some goal. The term comes from football, where a running game is an offense based on the ball-carrier's running with the ball rather than on passing. It began to be used figuratively from about 1965 on, as in "The National Science Foundation awarded a $61 million

grant to a consortium headed by Florida State University, ...
saying scientists at the Tallahassee institution were more
likely to 'run with the ball' than their competing counterparts
at the Massachusetts Institute of Technology" (*Boston Globe*,
Aug. 18, 1990).

safe by a mile
Totally secure; assured of success. The term comes from base-ball, where it signifies that a runner has reached a base well before he or she can be tagged out. The mile, of course, is pure hyperbole.

> "*Interpret what this goddamn cotton market is going to do tomorrow, and we can both quit chasing this blank blank sandlot ball team.*"
>
> —*Encounter*, Oct. 8, 1954

sandlot
Describing a rough or amateurish version of an activity. The term comes from *sandlot baseball*, so called since the 1880's for youngsters' baseball games (and other sports) played on vacant corner lots.

> "*The object of a bunker or trap is . . . also to punish pride and egotism.*"
>
> —CHARLES BLAIR MACDONALD, quoted in *Inside Golf*, eds. Bob Chieger and Pat Sullivan

sand trap
An obstacle or dilemma. The term comes from golf, where it denotes a shallow pit, partly sand-filled, deliberately located near a green so as to constitute a hazard. The term began to be used figuratively for any kind of hazard in the mid-20th century, as in "The new program seems to be full of sand traps for the computer novice."

saved by the bell
Rescued just in time. The bell here is the one that ends a round of boxing. If a fighter is down and it rings before the of-ficials reach the count of ten, he is not officially out of the

bout. (In some sets of rules, however, the count continues, whether or not the bell has rung.) The term began to be used figuratively for other last-minute reprieves in the mid-20th century.

say it ain't so, Joe

Tell me the worst is really not true. This expression became famous in 1919 during the so-called scandal of the "Black Sox," as the Chicago White Sox were referred to, in which the World Series was allegedly thrown by that team in order to accommodate gamblers. Supposedly it was uttered by a young fan to Shoeless Joe Jackson, the most famous of the players accused and brought before a grand jury. According to an item in the *Chicago Herald and Examiner*, Jackson answered, "Yes, kid, I'm afraid it is." The story must be deemed apocryphal, since Jackson always denied both his guilt and ever saying anything resembling this admission (a court acquitted him but he was permanently banned from baseball). Nevertheless, the expression survived. In 1987 it was revived when Senator Joseph Biden of Delaware dropped out of the race for the Democratic presidential nomination after being accused of plagiarism in his speeches, and again the following year when runner Ben Johnson of Canada was stripped of his Olympic gold medal after testing positive for steroid use.

> *"One needs a score card to keep track of chefs at Chelsea Central."*
>
> —Restaurant reviewer BRYAN MILLER,
> *New York Times,* Jan. 31, 1992

score

The final tally; the end result. The term has been used in sports and games since the 18th century, having been taken over from the innkeeper's tally of a customer's drinks. In the 20th century it came to be used figuratively for the essential result or crux of a matter, in such terms as to KNOW THE SCORE. The verb form, *to score,* which in sports means to score a touchdown, run, etc., has been used figuratively for any kind of gain or achievement since the late 19th century. In vulgar slang it also means to achieve sexual intercourse; for example, reporter Jane Gross wrote, ". . . using the local slang for sexual intercourse, which he says he has had 66 times, making him the group's top scorer" (*New York Times*, Mar. 29, 1993).

Further, to be *in scoring position*, meaning about to score a run or touchdown or whatever, is also used figuratively for someone about to succeed.

The 14th-century innkeeper's scorekeeping of customers' consumption generally involved marking a piece of wood or some other material with notches or other marks. Scorekeeping in sports such as baseball and cricket involves recording the statistics of a game on a *score card*, a term that was being used figuratively for other tallies and lists by the early 20th century. See also KNOW THE SCORE.

scratch, to
To eliminate or withdraw. Most authorities hold that the term comes from horse racing, where a horse that is scratched is one that has been withdrawn from a race. The *scratch sheet* is a publication that lists entries, withdrawals (or scratches), likely odds, jockeys, and weights for a day's races. These racing terms date from the mid-19th century. However, the term has an even longer history in the meaning of erasing a person's name from a list. In England it was used from the late 17th century on to mean expelling a member from a club, a usage now obsolete. And in America from 1847 or thereabouts, *to scratch a ticket* meant to strike out some of the names on a ballot. It is possible that the racing terminology came from these. See also START FROM SCRATCH.

screwball
An eccentric, zany individual. The term comes from baseball, where it denotes a breaking ball that breaks in the opposite way from a curve ball, that is, to the right when thrown by a right-handed pitcher and to the left when thrown by a southpaw. It is an extremely deceptive pitch but hard to control.

Among the first to use it successfully was Christy Mathewson of the New York Giants, about 1900, but it was not popularized until the reign of another Giants pitcher, Carl Hubbell. He pitched from 1928 to 1943 and is credited with giving the screwball its name about 1925. It began to be transferred to erratic or eccentric individuals in the 1930's.

> " 'Thataway,' he said, 'play the anthem and get the ball in the air. We're ready to scrimmage.' "
>
> —TOM KAKONIS, *Crisscross* (1990)

scrimmage, to

To engage in a rough or vigorous struggle or skirmish. The term comes from football, where *a scrimmage* denotes the head-on contact and tussle of play that begins with the snap at the LINE OF SCRIMMAGE (as distinct from that beginning with a free kick). It has a similar meaning in rugby and hence is familiar in Britain as well.

In American football *a scrimmage* also denotes a practice session in which a team divides itself into two sides and plays a game, so that "to scrimmage" can mean "to practice."

second, a

A person who helps or supports another. The term comes from boxing, where it denotes the assistants and advisers to a boxer between rounds. The boxing term in turn came from dueling, where it denoted a person who attended or represented the duelist.

> "Second-guessing is part of baseball. The fans get that right when they buy a ticket, or even if they don't."
>
> —YOGI BERRA, *It Ain't Over* (1989)

second-guessing

To criticize an event after the fact, with the benefit of hindsight. The term appears to have originated in the 1940's in baseball, where it designates after-the-game criticism of how a game was played, the decisions of umpires and coaches, and the like. About the same time it also was used in horse racing to mean predicting the outcome of a race, a usage that is less common. It soon was widely transferred to exercising twenty-twenty hindsight in any area or enterprise.

> *"When Graham played football at U.S.C. he never made first string. That bit of history stuck like a character trait; all his life he seemed to miss the crucial promotion, the next step up a detective's career."*
> —MICHAEL CRICHTON, *Rising Sun* (1992)

second-string
A substitute or second-best member of a group. This term may have originated in the practice of tethering horses on a single rope, but it came into popular usage in various team sports, where it denotes the second-best team or the substitutes, as opposed to the A TEAM.

second wind
A renewal of energy. The term comes from various sports, particularly running, where it describes what happens when a participant runs out of breath but then, after continuing, resumes regular breathing. In the early 1900's the term began to be used figuratively, as in Josephine Tey's mystery, *The Franchise Affair* (1946), "Perhaps it was the presence of an ally ... or perhaps she had just got her second wind."

send to the showers, to
To remove from action; to retire. The term comes from baseball, where a pitcher frequently is told to retire and make way for a substitute. The "showers," of course, is a metaphor for the locker room. The term was being transferred to other kinds of enterprise by about 1920.

set the pace, to
To establish a standard or a fashion. The term comes from horse racing, where it is said of a horse that goes out in front and leads the field. Such a horse is also called a *pacesetter*, and

both terms were being used figuratively by the early 20th
century. Closely related is the *pacemaker*, a jockey or rower
who sets the pace for another in racing or training for a race.
This term, of course, was transferred to the medical pacemaker, the device that supplies electrical signals to the heart
so as to maintain its regular beating.

seventh-inning stretch

A rest period; an intermission. The term comes from baseball,
where since the 1860's it has been customary to pause and allow spectators to rise and stretch their legs after six and one-
half innings have been played. There are various theories as
to how it became an institution. One, for example, is that
President William Howard Taft got up to stretch at this point
in a game in 1910, and the crowd rose with him as a sign of
respect. None has been verified, but the tradition continues,
and the term is occasionally used figuratively for other kinds
of pause or intermission.

> *"To fight with a shadow . . . passeth for the proverbial
> expression of a vain and useless act."*
> —THOMAS FULLER, *Appeal of Injured Innocence* (1659)

shadow boxing

Sparring with an imaginary adversary. Presumably the idea
behind this expression came from pugilism even back in the
16th century, when Shakespeare was one of several writers to
use it figuratively for a pointless activity. For prizefighters, of
course, it is a useful form of training. The precise modern
term came into being about 1900 and was used figuratively almost immediately. Sinclair Lewis had it in *Free Air* (1924),
"She fought the steering-wheel as though she were shadow-
boxing" (cited by *OED*).

"Taft Appears to Be Shoo-In for Top Senate G.O.P. Job"
—Headline, *Tuscaloosa News*, July 30, 1948

shoo-in

A sure thing. This term comes from horse racing and originally, from about 1900 on, meant a horse that was sure to win, because the race had been fixed beforehand by the jockeys (who of course bet on the winner). The word alludes to the fact that the winner is "shooed in"—that is, chased in—by the others. By about 1930 the term had been transferred to other events in which the outcome appeared to be a certainty. It was used particularly often for a candidate who seemed sure to win.

shoot the gap, to

To take advantage of an opening. The term comes from football, where it means to charge between opposing linemen to get at either the ball-carrier or the passer. In the late 20th century it began to be transferred to other enterprises, as in "The rush-hour subway crowd was impossible today—I had to shoot the gap to make my plane."

shot-making

A high rate of success. The term comes from basketball, where it refers to making a relatively large number of baskets per game, that is, a great many accurate placements. It began to be transferred to other kinds of success in the late 20th century, as in "The new superstore is a prime example of Bill's shot-making."

"Basketball has so much showboating you'd think it was invented by Jerome Kern."
—ART SPENDER, *Scholastic Coach*, Dec., 1983

showboat

An ostentatious person, a show-off. This term first designated a 19th-century riverboat, particularly a paddle-wheel steamer, used as a traveling theater and immortalized in Jerome Kern's 1927 musical comedy, *Show Boat*. It then began to be used for athletes who performed in a sensational manner designed to draw audience attention, and subsequently was transferred to any kind of show-off. It is also used in verb form, *to showboat*, meaning to show off, as in the quotation above.

shutout

Any contest in which the opponent cannot score, or where one side is particularly successful. The term originally was used in mid-19th-century American sports, particularly in baseball, for any game in which the opposing team had a score of zero. The baseball record for pitching shutouts belongs to Walter Johnson of the Washington Senators, who marked up 113 in a career of twenty-one years.

sideline, to: *see* ON THE SIDELINES.

sit on the ball, to

To behave defensively. The term comes from such sports as football, where it means to play conservatively when one's team is ahead in order to avoid giving the opponents an easy opportunity to score. In the late 20th century it began to be used figuratively, as in "They're sitting on the ball with the new product line in order to give the old ones maximum exposure."

sitting duck

An easy mark. The term comes from hunting, where it is of course much easier to shoot a stationary bird than one that is in flight (ducks attain speeds of 60 to 70 miles per hour). The term began to be used figuratively at the beginning of World War II, at first referring to the targets of enemy flak and bombs. It has since been extended to any easy target or vulnerable person, as in "Recently widowed, she was a sitting duck for an unscrupulous financial adviser."

sitting on the pole: *see* INSIDE TRACK.

skate, to

To progress quickly and easily. The term alludes to ice skating, in which the skate blades glide smoothly over a flat icy surface. It is used figuratively in such expressions as "She skated through the final exam." A similar figurative expression of the same provenance is *to skate over/around something*, meaning to avoid a subject, fact, etc., alluding to the skater passing quickly over or around an obstacle. See also SKATE ON THIN ICE.

"In skating over thin ice our safety is in our speed."
—RALPH WALDO EMERSON, *Prudence* (1841)

skate on thin ice, to

To place oneself in a delicate or risky position. The obvious source of this term is ice skating, and it alludes to the skater who takes the chance of falling through thin ice to the cold water under it. Emerson was among the first to use it figuratively, and nearly a century later the incorrigible Ogden Nash punned on it: "To indulge in a little bit of risquéting on thin ice" (*King Lear*, 1933).

> *"I just get out on the ice and skate the wing hard."*
>
> —JUDGE B. JOSEPH FITZSIMMONS, JR.,
> quoted in *Boston Globe*, Mar. 11, 1991

skate the wing hard, to

Vigorous, aggressive behavior. This term comes from ice hockey, where it means to put up an aggressive offense on the wing, that is, skate faster on either side (wing) of the center so as to score. In the late 20th century it and two related hockey terms, *go to the net* and *charge the goal*, meaning make an aggressive attempt to score, were used figuratively for other kinds of tough behavior. In the quotation above, the judge was defending himself against allegations of misconduct on the bench, maintaining that he expected to be exonerated of all charges and was simply hardworking, honest, and tough.

ski mask

A one-piece knitted hat and face covering, with holes for the eyes and mouth. Originally designed for skiers to protect the face against cold temperatures and icy winds on the slopes, in the second half of the 20th century it was increasingly used as a disguise by muggers and robbers, particularly in holdups. Although it continues in use as a cold-weather garment, the ski mask has become identified with its more nefarious purpose as well.

> *" 'I fear they assume this election will be a slam dunk,' Rollins said."*
>
> —*Boston Globe*, July 24, 1991

slam dunk

A particularly forceful move. The term comes from basketball, where it denotes a strong and often dramatic dunk shot, in which the player leaps up and thrusts the ball into the basket from above. Both the term and the technique date from the second half of the 20th century, when the increase in average height of professional basketball players enabled such shots to become less of a rarity. For example, in 1961 Wilt Chamberlain began the NBA season in which his scoring average was to be 50.4 points, many of which were scored by slam dunking.

From the mid-1980's on the term began to be transferred. Thus, a business consultant named to an important new job said of his reaction to being warned that companies might not accept advice from a black: "I found that very energizing. . . . There was a real opportunity to slam dunk that one" (reported by Paul Hemp, *Boston Globe*, May 5, 1992). The term has also been adopted in commercial aviation, referring to a technique whereby the plane stays above other air traffic until the last moment and then quickly drops to land.

slaphappy

Dizzy, exhilarated, cheerfully irresponsible. This term comes from boxing, where it is synonymous with PUNCH DRUNK, that is, befuddled from being hit in the head too hard and/or too often. It began to be transferred to similar behavior from other causes in the 1930's, and about the same time acquired renewed emphasis on the "happy" part of the term, that is, the meaning of carefree and casual. It continues to be used in both senses, the former seen in, for example, "That third martini made her slaphappy," and the latter in "Getting his diploma made him positively slaphappy."

slap shot

A vigorous blow. The term comes from ice hockey, where it denotes a powerful and rapid shot of the puck on the goal, made with a full swing of the stick. The expression began to be used metaphorically in the late 20th century, as in "That hostile witness really was a slap shot to our defense."

*"He made a couple of motion pictures . . . and they
were what is called sleepers. They made a lot of
money, considering what they cost."*

—JOHN D. MACDONALD, *Free Fall in Crimson* (1981)

sleeper

Something or someone whose value or ability is underestimated. The term as currently used comes from horse racing, where in the late 19th century it was used for a horse that performed far better than was expected (see also DARK HORSE). However, in the mid-19th century it was used with a somewhat different meaning in such card games as faro, where it signified a bet that the owner had forgotten and that therefore became public property.

By the early 20th century the word was being used figuratively in other areas, as for a play that proved to be an unexpected hit, an employee who did surprisingly well with a new project, etc.

*"Half a dozen of Rynders' sluggers immediately rushed
upon the brash youth."*

—HERBERT ASBURY, *Sucker's Progress* (1938)

slugger

A powerful person, one who behaves aggressively (verbally or physically); also, a semi-ironic term of endearment for a little boy or girl who tries to behave like one. The term has been used in baseball since the 19th century for a strong batter, as well as in boxing for a fighter known for delivering hard punches. It began to be used figuratively about 1900. The *Manchester Guardian Weekly* had it on Oct. 16, 1952: "Their team includes Mr Gromyko and the notorious slugger Vyshinsky" (cited by *OED*).

"In France they might have had a chance ... but here they were snookered."
— KENNETH GILES, *A Death in the Church* (1970)

snookered, to be

To be stymied or duped. The term comes from a variety of billiards called snooker, where it denotes being unable to shoot directly at the proper object ball because one or more other object balls are in the way. When snookered, the player must strike the proper object ball first, or he or she fouls. The term was transferred to other difficult situations by the early 20th century.

"The sport of skiing consists of wearing three thousand dollars' worth of clothes and equipment, and driving two hundred miles in the snow in order to stand around a bar and get drunk."
— P. J. O'ROURKE, *Modern Manners* (1983)

snow bunny

A woman who wears fashionable sportswear but spends most of her time socializing rather than on the ski slopes. The term dates from the second half of the 20th century and is occasionally transferred to other "groupies" who congregate about active participants in an activity without actually taking part themselves.

softball

An easy question or problem. The term alludes to the version of baseball called softball, which uses a larger, slightly softer ball than a baseball and is pitched underhand, with somewhat less force. The game began in 1857 as a form of indoor baseball and remains popular. See also PLAY HARDBALL.

sore loser: *see* POOR SPORT.

"No Contest Among Fetuses: Righties 212, Southpaws 12"

—Headline, *New York Times,* Nov., 1990

southpaw
A left-handed individual. This term allegedly was coined in Chicago in the 1880's because the Chicago Cubs' home plate faced east. When a left-handed pitcher faces west (home), his throwing arm is then to the south. The reason for this orientation supposedly was that during an afternoon game it kept the sun out of the batter's eyes as well as shielding the eyes of customers in the expensive seats behind home plate. Among the earliest writers to use the term were sportswriter

Charlie Seymour and humorist Finley Peter Dunne, but it is no longer certain who invented it. The term also gained acceptance in boxing, where it denotes a fighter who takes a stance with the right foot and arm leading and counterpunches with the left. Among the first great boxers known for this pattern was Gene Tunney, who decided to practice it after being defeated by Harry Greb. In the 1930's the term also was used occasionally for a left-wing politician, but this sense seems to have fallen into disuse.

Today "southpaw" means any kind of left-handed person, and because southpaws are in the minority—they represent about 10 percent of the population—numerous theories (and myths) have arisen concerning left-handedness. According to Stanley Coren, author of *The Left-Hander Syndrome* (1992), the superiority of southpaw batters is a myth, despite the success of Babe Ruth and Ted Williams, and what appears to have helped these peerless sluggers is that they were "right-eyed." Some advantages are nevertheless perceived, since managers tend to put left-handed pitchers against left-handed batters and vice versa. (Indeed, the name *southpaw disease* is used for the difficulty lefties often have in batting against lefty pitchers.) In any event, left- and right-handedness appear to be inherited traits, as a study of thumb-sucking fetuses suggests (see the headline quoted above). However, southpaws also appear to have a shorter lifespan, perhaps because their minority orientation makes them more apt to experience fatal accidents in a world where tools, machinery, etc., are made to accommodate the predominantly right-handed population.

spar, to
To argue or dispute. The term comes from the meaning of "spar" in boxing, which is to practice or train, often with a partner of similar build and style to that of a forthcoming opponent. Indeed, this person is called a *sparring partner.* The verb has been transferred to figurative kinds of fighting since about 1700. The term "sparring partner" dates only from about 1900 and has been used figuratively since the mid-20th

century for a person with whom one enjoys arguing (and, humorously, for one's mate or spouse).

"Sport is sweetest when there be no spectators."
—JOHN CLARKE, *Paroemiologia* (1639)

spectator sport
An activity that one observes as opposed to one in which one participates. The term has been used since about 1940 for sports such as football and ice hockey, for which numerous onlookers are willing to pay a fee (and which require too high a level of expertise to engage a large number of participants). In the second half of the 20th century the term began to be transferred, often ironically, to nonathletic activities, as in "Voter turnout has been so poor that this election has become a spectator sport."

"I don't know if he throws a spitball but he sure spits on the ball."
—Yankees manager CASEY STENGEL,
about an opposing pitcher

spitball
A dirty trick; a deceptive action. The term comes from baseball, where it denotes a pitch thrown much like a fastball but with the ball or fingers moistened with saliva. The moisture causes the ball to slip from the fingers with little rotation and break sharply downward as it nears the plate. Once a legal tactic, the spitball was officially banned in 1920, although a species of grandfather clause permitted practicing spitballers to continue using it until they retired. The last spitball legally thrown was pitched by Burleigh Grimes in 1934. However, pitchers continue to use it surreptitiously to the present day. Earl Weaver said about Gaylord Perry's spitball, "We used to walk up and down the dugout saying, 'Forget about it, hit the dry side.' He'd throw it twice and you'd be looking for it on 116 pitches."

The spitball of baseball dates from the mid-19th century. Also from this period comes the use of the identical word for the ancient schoolroom trick of using small wads of chewed-up paper as missiles.

The transfer of spitball to other kinds of deceptive weapon dates from the last decades of the 19th century.

split decision
A verdict in which there is some dissent. The term comes from boxing, where it denotes the decision of a bout made on points, because the officials are not unanimous in their choice of the winner. The term dates from the mid-20th century and is occasionally transferred to other situations in which there is disagreement concerning an outcome—for example, "The town meeting came to a split decision concerning the budget override."

sport, a
One who plays by the rules. See GOOD LOSER/SPORT; SPORTSMANSHIP. This noun has numerous other meanings as well: a particular form of athletics, involving skill, physical prowess, a set of rules, and the like; an amusing pastime or diversion; a flashy dresser or bon vivant. The meaning of pleasant entertainment and, by extension, a joke or ridicule, dates from the 15th century and survives in such expressions as *to make sport of* (i.e., to make fun of something or someone). "For what do we live, but to make sport for our neighbours and laugh at them in our turn?" wrote Jane Austen in *Pride and Prejudice* (1813). The athletic sense dates from the 16th century, and that of an ostentatious person is of 19th-century American provenance. In 18th-century America a *sportsman* also was a professional gambler, a term that in the 19th century was sometimes altered to *sporting man* or *sporting gentleman*. M. James's 1833 biography of Andrew Jackson had it: "Sporting men were willing to wager that the deposits would be removed."

See also the entries beginning with "sport" that follow.

sporting chance
A fair opportunity for a favorable result. The term alludes to the uncertain outcome associated with any competitive sport,

and has been used in this way since about 1900. Mary H. Kingsley had it in *Travels in West Africa* (1897), "One must diminish dead certainties to the level of sporting chances" (cited by *OED*).

sports car

A small, low, streamlined automobile, usually seating only two persons and with an engine quite powerful relative to the car's size. Basically an imitation of a racing car but intended for use on public roads, it is designed with such racing-car features as quick response and acceleration, maneuverability, and precise handling. The term dates from the 1920's, when such cars began to be built. The cars actually used in racing differ in that the engine is always in the rear, there is only a driver's seat, and such highway equipment as headlights and windshield wipers are omitted. Racing cars compete in classes depending on engine displacement.

"Playing a cheater is the real test of sportsmanship."
—JACK BARNABY, *Winning Squash Racquets* (1979)

sportsmanship

Ethical behavior in any area of competition (business, government, etc.). The term comes from such behavior in athletics, which includes courtesy toward one's opponent, refusal to take unfair advantage of a situation, and graciousness in winning and losing. Originally sportsmanship simply meant engaging in an athletic activity, but since the 18th century it has signified doing so fairly and graciously. The idea, of course, is much older. In ancient Rome, Cicero wrote, "I care not who makes the laws or even writes the songs if the code of sportsmanship is sound, for it is that which controls conduct and governs the relationship between men."

Unsportsmanlike conduct, in contrast, includes giving unfair assistance to a player, deliberately distracting an opponent, fighting, using profanity or abusive language, striking an official, and gloating when one wins and sulking when one loses. In numerous sports, unsportsmanlike conduct is now penalized. In basketball it is punished with a technical foul, and in lacrosse with a personal foul. In football the team may be penalized a number of yards, and/or the offending player disqualified. In track and field the player is disqualified. And in professional tennis tournaments the player may incur warnings, loss of points (up to the loss of the match), and fines for such offenses as ball abuse, racket abuse, bad language, etc. See also GOOD LOSER/SPORT; POOR SPORT.

> *"The spring-board whence she took her next leap into the arena of insolence."*
>
> —E. LYNN LINTON, *The Autobiography of Christopher Kirkland* (1885)

springboard
A point of departure; an impetus or launching for a beginning or change. The term probably originated in gymnastics in the late 18th century. Henry David Thoreau refers to one used by tumblers in a journal entry of 1841, an elastic board to assist in vaulting. A similar device is used in diving. For competitive diving it consists of a flexed and springy platform, either one or three meters above the water surface. In both activities it serves to increase the height of the performer's leaps. The word has been used figuratively since the early 20th century.

> *"Another time in spring training . . . the clubhouse man asked me what size hat I wore. I told him I was not in shape yet."*
>
> —YOGI BERRA, *It Ain't Over* (1989)

spring training
A preliminary event or practice period during which the results do not count. The term comes from baseball, where it denotes an approximately six-weeks-long season for training and exhibition games. It dates from the late 19th century. In the late 20th century it was sometimes used figuratively, as in "The presidential primaries are really a form of spring training."

"The true sprinter is, by nature, necessity, and training, a physical spendthrift."
—BRIAN MITCHELL, *Athletics Weekly*, Aug. 19, 1972

sprint

A short spell of vigorous activity. The term comes from various kinds of racing—track, rowing, etc.—in which it denotes moving at full speed for a short distance. Often it refers to a burst of all-out speed near the finish line. The word has been used figuratively since the late 19th century, as in "There is too much of a 'sprint' in the last act" (*Westminster Gazette*, Oct. 23, 1895; cited by *OED*).

"Most employers of relatively small numbers of workers . . . appear to have been caught in an economic squeeze play."
—*Baltimore Sun*, Sept. 14, 1932

squeeze play

Applying pressure on an individual or group in order to gain an advantage. The term seems to have originated in baseball about 1900. It denotes a prearranged play in which the runner on third base breaks for home on the pitch and the batter bunts. In a slightly different form, called a *safety squeeze play*, the runner waits until the batter has actually bunted. The term was being used figuratively by about 1915 and continues in current usage; Jane Leary used it as the title of her 1990 novel.

stalking horse

A pretext; something put forward to conceal one's true motive, the true candidate for office, etc. The term comes from hunting and dates from the early 16th century, when hunters would actually dismount and hide behind their horses to stalk game on foot until they got close enough to get a good shot. Occasionally they used a figure of a horse rather than the actual animal. By the late 16th century the term had been transferred to other kinds of pretense, as it still is. In 1992 several states, including Connecticut and Massachusetts, passed a *stalking law*, which set a mandatory prison sentence for a person convicted of following or threatening another person while under a restraining order. Within a week of its passage it was invoked in two cases, both involving a man accused of stalking a woman who considered his presence harassment and had obtained a restraining order.

start from scratch, to
To begin from the very beginning, with no special advantage, knowledge, or influence. The term comes from various kinds of race in which the starting point is a line scratched on the ground. (One writer maintains that at the very first Olympic Games, held in Greece in 776 B.C., the beginning point of a race was a line scratched in the sand.) The term has been used figuratively since about 1920. See also COME UP TO SCRATCH; SCRATCH.

> "*Emanuel Ax played this concerto with skill and taste ... (Conductor) Krainer left him at the starting gate.*"
> —RICHARD DYER, *Boston Globe,* May 1, 1990

starting gate, (at) the
The proper place to begin for all competitors, so that none has an unfair advantage. The term comes from various kinds of racing. In horse racing it consists of a mechanical removable barrier made of strands of rope that fly up when a catch is pressed to release them. In harness racing it consists of a lever system of arms extending from a specially constructed car that moves along. In skiing, on the other hand, it is a fixed point from which individual runs are timed. Whatever its mechanics, the starting gate is designed to ensure an equal start for all competitors. In the late 20th century the term was used figuratively, as in the quotation above, where music critic Dyer points out that the conductor raced ahead of the soloist in this performance. In this usage, to be *left at the starting gate* is synonymous with being LEFT AT THE POST.

stay the course, to

To last or hold out until the end. The term has been used since the late 19th century in horse racing, where it refers to a horse's endurance for the entire length of the race. It began to be transferred to other enterprises in the first half of the 20th century, as in "He's having a hard time with his dissertation topic, but I'm sure he'll stay the course."

> *"The problem of who sits where in the front family pews when there have been divorces and remarriages can create a sticky wicket."*
>
> —LETITIA BALDRIDGE, special wedding supplement,
> *New York Times*, June 14, 1992

sticky wicket

A difficult situation. The term comes from cricket, where "wicket" has two meanings: (1) one of two sets of three vertical stumps on which are placed two horizontal wooden strips, or bails, which the bowler tries to knock down and which the batsman defends (by hitting the ball that is bowled at them); and (2) the 22-yard-long pitch (strip of grass) between the stumps and bails (at either end of the field), over which the batsmen run in order to score points. It is the latter kind of wicket to which the term refers. Specifically, a sticky wicket is a pitch that is drying out in the sun after having been soaked with rain. It is temporarily tacky and favors the bowler (over the batsman) because the ball "bites" into the drying turf, giving it extra spin.

Cricket was introduced into the United States in the mid-18th century and was quite popular for more than a hundred years, but it was superseded by baseball from the 1860's on. Nevertheless, this particularly cricket term caught on and is used figuratively in America, although less often than in those English-speaking countries where cricket remains very popular.

stiff-arm, to

Also, *straight-arm*. To fend off, rebuff, or reject. The term comes from football, where it means to hold off a would-be tackler by extending one's arm straight out. Although offensive players are not allowed to use the hands to ward off or stop defensive players, a ball-carrier in danger of being tackled may shove out his hand to the side or rear in a straight jabbing motion to push away the tackler. The term dates from the early 20th century and was being used figuratively by about 1935, both as a verb and as an adjective, as in, for example, "Countervening such stiff-arm tactics as the lynch law with sit-ins and other peaceful demonstrations was not going to work."

stonewall, to

To block, delay, or otherwise resist. Although in America during the Civil War this term became a nickname for General Thomas J. Jackson (1824–63) of the Confederate Army, for his reluctance to surrender any position to the enemy, the verb form became familiar through cricket, where it means the unsporting practice of playing for time. From there it was transferred (in Britain) to stalling or obstructing legislation, especially by means of a filibuster. And in the 20th century it returned to America to be used in both political and nonpolitical contexts for stalling and other forms of stubborn resistance. *Newsweek* used it during the Watergate affair that brought down President Richard Nixon: "The President himself ... served notice that he would stonewall any further demands for tapes in the Watergate scandal" (May 11, 1974).

> "*Give me a chap that hits straight out from the shoulder.*"
> —CHARLES READE, *It Is Never Too Late to Mend* (1856)

straight from the shoulder

Absolutely direct and straightforward. The term comes from boxing, where it denotes a punch delivered straight, with full body weight behind it. It began to be used figuratively for other kinds of straightforwardness from about 1850 on.

stranglehold

A force that restricts another's free actions, ideas, or development. The term comes from wrestling, where it denotes any hold across the throat that would impede breathing. All such holds are illegal. The term has been used figuratively since the first half of the 20th century, as in "The new state regulations for women's health clinics put a stranglehold on the right-to-choose movement."

> "And it's one, two, three strikes you're out
> At the old ball game."
> —JACK NORWORTH, *Take Me Out to the Ball Game* (1908)

strike(s) against, to have a/two

To labor under a handicap or other drawback. The term comes from baseball, where a strike is a fairly pitched ball that the batter cannot successfully hit. Because the batter is allowed three strikes before being counted out, the precise wording of the metaphor varies. Thus, "She's got two strikes against her" means she is in a precarious position. Similarly, "That's a strike against him" means that he has one drawback (so far). See also STRIKE OUT; THREE STRIKES AGAINST YOU.

> "But there is no joy in Mudville—
> Mighty Casey has struck out."
> —ERNEST LAWRENCE THAYER, *Casey at the Bat* (1888)

strike out, to

Also, *strikeout*. To fail; a failure. The term comes from baseball, where a batter who fails to get a fair hit from three pitches in the strike zone is retired. While of course strikeouts are bad for the offensive team, they are a great plus for the defense, especially the pitcher, and strikeout records are avidly kept. The pitcher still credited with the most strikeouts was Walter Johnson, who pitched for the Washington Sena-

tors from 1907 to 1927. In 802 games he achieved 3,508 strikeouts. Another National League record was set by St. Louis
Cardinals pitcher Dizzy Dean on July 30, 1933, when he
struck out seventeen consecutive batters. He reportedly said,
"Heck, if anybody told me I was settin' a record I'd of got me
some more strikeouts" (quoted by Mel Allen and Frank Graham, Jr., *It Takes Heart*, 1959). The term was being transferred to other endeavors by about 1900, as in "That new
brand of soft drink struck out in all the stores." It is also put
as *to strike out with* something or someone, as in "She struck
out with her blind date."

> *"If the Dartmouth reporter wants to use my name in
> the headline of a story about a long meeting, that's
> fine. I think it is like reaching for a pitch out of the strike
> zone."*
>
> —YOGI BERRA, *It Ain't Over* (1989)

strike zone

The precise target area. The term comes from baseball, where
it denotes an imaginary rectangle over home plate from the
batter's knees to the armpits. A ball pitched into this area is
automatically called a strike, whether or not the batter
swings at it. During World War II the term was used to denote a target area for bombers and other forces, and since
then it has been extended to still more figurative usage, as in
"He's asking $2,500 for that old car; even if it were worth it,
that's way out of my strike zone."

stymie, to

To obstruct or thwart. This term comes from golf, where it
describes the situation where another ball lands on the green
directly between a player's ball and the hole, so that the
player cannot putt. The golfer then would have to use an iron
to make the ball jump over the intervening ball, or put spin on
the ball to make it curve around it. In 1951, however, the rules
were changed and players were permitted to mark the position of balls on the green, allowing them to remove the inter-

vening ball temporarily while they putted. By then the
figurative use of the word was well established, as in President George Bush's speech of September, 1990: "No longer
can a dictator count on East-West confrontation to stymie
U.N. action against aggression."

> *"Here was my quarterback in sudden-death overtime,
> and he's thinking about the fans getting their money's
> worth."*
>
> —JOHN MADDEN, *Hey, Wait a Minute* (1984)

sudden death

Settling a tie with a single stroke. The term comes from a variety of sports. In football, if there is a tie at the end of the
second half of a championship game, play must continue until
one side wins by scoring through a safety, field goal, or touchdown (this is called *sudden-death overtime*). The same rule
applies in soccer and ice hockey, that is, in case of a tie, the
team that scores first wins.

In golf a *sudden-death round* begins from a designated
hole—for example, the fifteenth—and continues until one
player wins by playing a hole in fewer strokes. During the
1985 New South Wales Open at Canberra, a local funeral di-
rector playing on the name offered a special prize for a hole-
in-one at the eighth hole: it was either 5,000 pounds or a
prepaid funeral with a monument. If a playoff became necessary, the eighth hole would be used for the sudden-death
playoff.

In tennis the term is used for a *tiebreaker* in which
twelve points are played, and the first to score seven points
wins, provided the seven exceed the opponent's score by two
points (7–5 is a winning score; at 7–6, play continues until the
winner has two more points than the loser). Occasionally a
nine-point tiebreaker is used, but only rarely in tournament
play. The term was transferred to other kinds of instantane-
ous decision in the late 20th century. Rita Mae Brown used
Sudden Death as the title of her 1983 novel.

"If you argue with Dave the Dude too much he is apt to reach over and lay his Sunday punch on your snoot."

—DAMON RUNYON, *Cosmopolitan*, Oct., 1929

Sunday punch

A powerful blow, literal or figurative. The term has been used in boxing since the 1920's for a boxer's best, strongest punch, especially the one used in trying for a knockout. John Ciardi suggested that it came from the analogy to one's "Sunday best," that is, the dress attire one saved for church and other special occasions, as opposed to everyday work clothes, and "also, whimsically, the punch with which he [the fighter] puts his opponent 'to rest with the Lord, his labors done.'" Fanciful as this last thought may be, the term was transferred to other kinds of powerful blow by the mid-20th century. W. W.

Elton had it in his *Guide to Naval Aviation* (1944): "The real 'Sunday punch' of naval aviation is the torpedo bomber" (cited by *OED*).

Super Bowl

A final contest between the outstanding contenders. The term alludes to the Super Bowl of football, the championship game between the best teams of the National Football Conference and the American Football Conference respectively. This Super Bowl has been held annually since 1967, when the Green Bay Packers defeated the Kansas City Chiefs in Los Angeles. In the late 20th century, the term was gradually transferred to other competitions determining a final champion, at first in other sports (Super Bowl of Bowling, Roller Skating, etc.) and then to nonathletic contests, such as spelling bees.

swimmer's ear

A bacterial infection in the ear canal, technically called external otitis. Its common name comes from the fact that it tends to afflict swimmers, especially those who swim outdoors during the summer months. Its symptoms include itching, pain, a foul-smelling discharge, and, if there is swelling in the canal, hearing loss.

swing for the fences, to

To go all-out in any endeavor. The term comes from baseball and refers to a batter's attempt to hit a home run, the fences being those of the ballpark. In the second half of the 20th century it began to be used figuratively for other all-out efforts, as in "In this new advertising campaign the whole agency is swinging for the fences."

switch-hitter

A person who radically alternates his or her orientation in opinions, activities, behavior, sexual preference, etc. The term comes from baseball, where since the 1930's it has described a player who bats either right- or left-handed. One of the most famous switch-hitters in baseball history was New York Yankees outfielder Mickey Mantle, who became famous for hitting extremely long home runs. He led the American League in home runs four times and hit eighteen World Series homers; in addition, he was valued for his ability to drive in runs when they were most needed. The first switch-hitter to get 100 hits on each side in the same season was Garry Templeton of the St. Louis Cardinals; he did so in 1979, when he had a .314 batting average for the season.

The term began to be transferred to other kinds of more or less drastic alternation in the mid-20th century, and became a slang word for bisexuals about 1960.

swordplay

Skillful argument. The term comes from fencing, where it has been a synonym for the art and technique of wielding a sword for almost a thousand years (the *OED*'s earliest citation is dated approximately A.D. 1000). In the 19th century it was used figuratively for particularly clever verbal fighting—that is, expert debate.

T T T T T

> *"Football is only two things, blocking and tackling,"*
> —Attributed to football coach VINCE LOMBARDI

tackle, to

To come to grips with or deal with something or someone; to undertake or handle some problem or issue. Originally the word "tackle"—in both noun and verb forms—concerned the rigging of a ship, but in the mid-19th century the verb began to be used colloquially for physical encounters, such as wrestling holds, and in the latter half of the 19th century it became closely associated with soccer, rugby, and football. In soccer, tackling involves blocking an opponent in order to dislodge or otherwise win control of the ball. In football and rugby, it means to throw or knock the ball-carrier to the ground, or hold him in order to stop his progress. It is this sports meaning of vigorously taking hold of something or someone that is most often transferred today, as in "We've got to tackle these witnesses one by one, or we'll never find out what really happened."

> *" 'Do you intend to go through your pregnancy and delivery alone?' ... 'I've already talked to Hilda and Racine,' Vivian said. 'They'll be my tag-team partners.' "*
> —LOUISE ERDRICH and MICHAEL DORRIS,
> *The Crown of Columbus* (1991)

tag team

A group or pair whose members assist each other in some enterprise. The term comes from wrestling, where it denotes a team of two or more professional wrestlers who spell each other during a match. In the 1970's the term began to be extended to such sports as ice hockey (as in "This [hockey] game now turned into a six-man tag-team match") and in the 1990's to other enterprises altogether, as in the quotation above.

take a hike
Go away, you're not wanted here. This impolite American imperative refers to the outdoor sport of walking a fair distance over rough terrain. However, it is alluding to the distance rather than to any pleasure derived from the activity. The word "hike" has been used in America for what the British call a "tramp" or "ramble" since the early 19th century. The rude imperative, however, dates only from the second half of the 20th century.

take a rain check: *see* RAIN CHECK.

take the count: *see* DOWN BUT NOT OUT.

talk a good game, to
To speak or act very knowledgeably, even though (or particularly when) one is not. This term clearly originated in one or another sport, although the precise origin has been lost. Generally used with some scorn, it describes a player who either knows a great deal about the rules, tactics, and the like, or pretends to, even though he or she is not particularly outstanding in performance. In use since the mid-20th century, it has been transferred to just about any endeavor where a person's performance is being questioned, as in "He talks a good game, but he's actually a terrible cook."

tank, to
To lose deliberately. The term comes from a slightly older one from boxing, to *go in the tank*, which means to go through the motions of a fight but lose by prearrangement, usually because of heavy wagers placed on the opponent's winning. The precise wording of the boxing term is believed to have evolved from the still older term, to *take a dive* (to the canvas). It was extended to other sports in the mid-20th century, but the "go in the" part was dropped and the noun changed to

a verb. Tanking is, of course, illegal, no matter what sport is involved. In the late 20th century it was sometimes used figuratively, as in "The candidate was canceling one press conference after another, so the reporters thought he was tanking it." See also SAY IT AIN'T SO, JOE.

> *"It ain't the individual, nor the army as a whole,*
> *But the everlastin' teamwork of every bloomin' soul."*
> —Attributed to J. MASON KNOX, *Cooperation* (1918)

teamwork

A coordinated effort to achieve a common end. The word *team* itself was first used for work animals such as oxen or horses that were harnessed so as to pull together. By the 17th century it had been transferred to people drawing together for one reason or another, particularly for a concerted effort. Although the word "teamwork" was long used for the labors of an animal team, it only began to be used for the efforts of an athletic team around 1900. It was the sports meaning that quickly was transferred to other group endeavors, especially in the armed forces (as in the quotation above) and in business. A person who worked well with others was called a *team player*, and executives called on their subordinates to show *team spirit* (much as coaches do). In the late 1980's an American food company, Domino's Pizza, carried these sports metaphors even further, according to William Lutz's *Doublespeak* (1989). It described its staff not as employees but as "team members" (i.e., workers), "team leaders" (middle managers), and "coaches" (top management).

In the 1960's educators developed the concept of *team teaching*, a program in which two or more teachers integrate their subjects into a single course and together teach the students.

In Britain a team participating in a match is more often known as a "side" (see LET THE SIDE DOWN).

*"I thought you were about to tee off on Ben. . . . Let's
both stop making cracks."*
                            —HENRY KURNITZ, *Invasion of Privacy* (1955)

tee(d) off, to (be)

To strike hard or severely scold; to be angry. This term comes
from golf, where to tee off means to begin play by hitting the
ball off the tee. At first it was transferred, with slightly different meanings, to several other sports. In boxing *to tee off
on* means to put all one's power in a punch; in baseball it
means either to bat a pitched ball a considerable distance, or
to make many runs and hits. The golf term dates from the
17th century. The other sports usages arose during the first
half of the 20th century, as do the figurative ones, which remain largely American colloquialisms. For example, "She teed
off on her son for borrowing the car without permission"
means she hit him with a severe scolding, rather than striking
actual blows. At the same time, "the boy's behavior really
teed off his mother" means that he made her extremely angry.
The *OED* suggests the latter usage may have originated as a
euphemism for "peed off," or "pissed off," but cites no verification for this hypothesis.

*"I arrived late, in the orthodox costume—that is to say,
a straw hat which is oftener off than on, a flannel shirt
two sizes too large for me, and a pair of flannels."*
                      —F. B. DOVETON, "At a Lawn Tennis Party,"
                                  A Fisherman's Fancies (1895)

Tennis, anyone?

Also, *Who's for tennis?* A humorous non sequitur. This term
originated as a stock line in British comedies of about 1910 to
1940, which featured a country-house setting, upper-class
characters devoted to leisure, and the old-fashioned garb described in the quotation above. It therefore became an ironic
comment on the idle rich, but by the time it crossed the Atlantic, roughly after World War II, it simply signified a ridic-
ulous non sequitur. A 1969 *New Yorker* cartoon pictures a

stage with a group of nude men and women, one of whom
waves a tennis racket and asks the others, "Tennis, anyone?"

> *"Tennis elbow isn't confined to persons who play
> racket sports. We treated a violinist who had tennis el-
> bow in his left arm . . . a man who had to use a screw-
> driver on his job. . . ."*
>
> —HANS KRAUS, *Sports Injuries* (1981)

tennis elbow

A strain of the lateral forearm muscles or their tendon attach-
ments, technically called lateral humeral epicondylitis. The
popular name dates from the 1880's and comes from the fact
that the disorder frequently afflicts tennis players, but it also
occurs in individuals who play no sports whatever. The violinist mentioned in the quotation above forced his ear down to
the violin, producing tightness and tenderness down the arm.
Any movements that cause repetitive strenuous supination of
the wrist against resistance, as in operating a manual screw-
driver, or violent extension of the wrist with the hand pro-
nated, as in tennis, can cause the condition. As Billie Jean
King said, "Tennis is a perfect combination of violent action
taking place in an atmosphere of complete tranquility," so it is
hardly surprising that players suffer injury (*Billie Jean*, 1974).

Two comparable syndromes are *golfer's elbow*, involving
forearm muscle fibers, and *fly-caster's elbow*, a tendonitis similar to tennis elbow. John Gierach wrote about it in the *New
York Times*: "I had a lingering case of fly-caster's elbow. . . . I
think I got the elbow trouble in Texas in April while fighting
big bass on a nine-weight fly rod" (Dec. 2, 1992).

textbook play

A feat executed with virtually perfect form or technique. Ad-
miringly applied to, for example, a football play or series of
tennis shots, the term is clearly metaphoric, since there is
nothing equivalent to a standard text for these or any other
sports. Incidentally, in earlier times the adjective "textbook"
was more derogatory than flattering, meaning that the thing

so described was only mediocre or stereotyped. About the mid-20th century this implication was reversed to the commonly used current one of approbation, as in "Mary has really learned to drive well; that U-turn was a textbook play."

The man who complains about the way the ball bounces is likely the one who dropped it."
—Football coach LOU HOLTZ, quoted in
Los Angeles Times, Dec. 13, 1978

That's the way the ball bounces
That's fate; that's how things are, and there's nothing you can do about it. This catch phrase became extremely popular in the 1950's, along with such companions as "That's the way the cookie crumbles." Just what sport it originally alluded to is not known, but certainly a badly bounced ball can cause a player to make an error in numerous sports—baseball, tennis, golf, to name just a few. In some sports it is possible to avoid the consequences of a bad bounce by hitting or catching the ball before it bounces, but that, too, can have its hazards. In tennis it may mean that one is hitting a ball that would otherwise be out (and doubles partners frequently warn each other when one is about to hit a questionable ball on the fly, saying, "Bounce it"). Even this term has been used metaphorically, and as long ago as 1625, when James Howell, writing about marriage in a letter, said, "It concerns you not to be over-hasty herein, not to take the ball before the bound."

there's the rub: *see* RUB OF THE GREEN.

thoroughbred
Upper-class and aristocratic, well born and well bred. The term comes from horse racing, where it denotes a horse specifically bred for speed. In contrast to *purebred*, thoroughbred denotes a breed developed in Britain and Ireland during the 17th and 18th centuries. It is a direct descendant in the male line from three Arabian stallions imported into England during this period: the Byerly Turk, a military charger imported

in 1689; the Darley Arabian, in 1704; and the Godolphin Barb, taken from France to England about 1730. These stallions were mated with English mares, resulting in the Thoroughbred breed. The direct line actually survives only through a single descendant of each of them: Herod, from Byerly Turk; Eclipse, from the Darley Arabian; and Matchem, from the Godolphin Barb.

The term began to be used as a complimentary assessment of human beings in the late 19th century. Helen H. Gardener had it in *An Unofficial Patriot* (1894), "There is rather a paucity of thoroughbreds among the Methodists" (cited by *OED*).

.300 hitter/class/man

An expert. The term comes from baseball, where it denotes a player with a .300 BATTING AVERAGE, which is very good indeed. It has been used figuratively, although not with great frequency, since about 1900.

> *"Baseball is almost the only orderly thing in a very unorderly world. If you get three strikes, even the best lawyer in the world can't get you off."*
>
> —BILL VEECK, Chicago White Sox owner

three strikes against you, to have

To have no chance whatever; to lose. The term comes from baseball, where a batter is retired after three pitched balls are called strikes, whether or not he swung at them. It began to be used figuratively from the late 19th century on. See also STRIKE(S) AGAINST.

throw in the sponge/towel, to

To give up. The term comes from boxing, where fighters (or their seconds) formerly conceded defeat by throwing the towel or sponge used to wipe their faces from the boxer's corner into the ring. The term has been used figuratively since about 1900 and continues to be current, even though the actual practice is largely obsolete.

*"How if she . . . wished to throw my poor friend off the
scent by this false announcement."*
—MARY E. BRADDON, *Lady Audley's Secret* (1862)

throw off the scent, to

Also, to *put off the scent.* To evade or elude someone or something. The term comes from hunting, where the quarry—
especially a fox—may try to throw the pursuing hounds off
the scent. Certain conditions favor the hounds in that they
make the quarry's scent more pronounced: when the ground is
warmer than the air; after a sudden drop in temperature, just
before a frost; at night and in the early morning; on moist
ground; when the air is humid and in fog; and so on. The term
has been transferred to other kinds of evasion since the
mid-19th century.

*"My hat's in the ring. The fight is on and I'm stripped to
the buff."*
—THEODORE ROOSEVELT, interview at
Cleveland, Ohio, Feb. 21, 1912

throw one's hat in the ring, to

Also, *toss one's hat in the ring.* To enter a contest or announce
one's candidacy. The term comes from boxing, where throwing
a hat into the ring once signified a challenge. John Ciardi re-
peats a story about heavyweight champion John L. Sullivan,
who after an exhibition bout with sparring partners would
sometimes throw his hat in the ring as a challenge to all com-
ers, offering a prize to anyone who could stay upright with
him for a specified length of time. The term dates from the
early 19th century and was used figuratively from about 1900
on. Today it nearly always signifies political candidacy.

*"If we were behind in the last minute of a close game,
I always wanted to be able to use all three of my time-
outs. With all three, my quarterback could complete
three passes down the middle and stop the clock in-*

stead of being limited to throwing deep or to the side-line."

—JOHN MADDEN, *One Knee Equals Two Feet* (1986)

time out

Also, *time-out, timeout.* A suspension of activity; an intermission or pause. The term originated in the late 19th century in various American sports where it signified, as it still does, a short interruption in a regular period of play where the officials stop the clock. Time outs are called for purposes of rest, substitution, and the like. In football a time out is a 1.5-minute suspension of play required and charged to either team when the ball is dead; each team may have three time outs per half. In baseball a time out is a temporary suspension of play called by the umpire. In ice hockey each team is allowed a thirty-second stop per game, which may be taken only during normal stoppage of play. Similar rules govern other sports.

The term began to be used figuratively for any kind of break in activity in the first half of the 20th century. John D. Macdonald had it in his mystery, *Girl, Gold Watch, and Everything* (1962), "Everybody's in such a damn hurry, sugar, it's good for them to take some time out."

Tinker-to-Evers-to-Chance

A perfectly executed maneuver. The term refers to Joe Tinker, John Evers, and Frank Chance, who played in the Chicago Cubs infield from 1903 to 1913. Their skill in making double plays became legendary, and their names became permanently associated with it. Ironically, shortstop Joe Tinker and second baseman Johnny Evers hated each other. They originally had been good friends, but one day in 1908 Tinker got upset when Evers took a taxi to the ballpark and did not offer his friend a ride. The two quarreled and stopped speaking. For the next five years, until Tinker was traded to a different team, they continued their excellent fielding but spoke only on the field and then only when absolutely necessary. The silence finally was broken in 1930, when they ran into each other at a Chicago radio station and made up their quarrel.

"Tell him he can have my title but I want it back in the morning."
—Attributed to JACK DEMPSEY, answering
a drunk who challenged him

titleholder
The acknowledged champion. The term comes from boxing, where it has been used for the winners of championships since the late 19th century. Today the only generally accepted titleholders are in the heavyweight division, which in fact is the one that always has attracted the most attention and support. The term has been used figuratively since about 1900.

"At least four-fifths of those which get any sort of toe-hold in the language originate in the United States."
—H. L. MENCKEN, *The American Language* (1945)

toehold
A position of very slight advantage or support, giving one a bare start. The term is used in several sports, but this metaphor comes from climbing, where a toehold is a small crack, niche, or ledge that just barely supports the toe of the climber's boot. The term began to be used figuratively about 1900. In wrestling, incidentally, a toehold is an illegal hold involving bending or twisting the opponent's foot or toes.

"My colleague is afraid to 'toe the scratch' and take a vote directly on the question."
—Congressman SAM J. RANDALL,
Congressional Globe, Mar. 19, 1868

toe the line/mark/scratch, to
To abide strictly by the rules; to take one's responsibilities seriously. The term originated in racing, where the line, mark, or scratch signified the starting point (see START FROM SCRATCH). By about 1800 standing with one's toes at this line was being used figuratively, first in the sense of being ready for something and then, less directly, to signify conforming to something.

toe-to-toe

In direct confrontation; evenly matched. The term comes from boxing, where it signifies an exchange of punches in which the boxers face each other and slug away, without making any effort to move or defend themselves. By the mid-20th century the term was being used figuratively for other kinds of confrontation, as in "In the toe-to-toe fight for the Republican Presidential nomination, last week's round went to Senator Robert A. Taft of Ohio" (*Newsweek*, June 23, 1952).

touch (all) base(s), to

To make contact; to cover all the possibilities. Both versions of this term come from baseball, where touching a base is, of course, essential if a runner wants to be ruled as reaching it safely, and touching all bases means one has succeeded in scoring a run. Both terms began to be used figuratively after 1950. Clay Ford combined both senses in one in a book review, "He seems to have touched base with every active group" (*Saturday Review*, July 22, 1974).

touché

You've got me/it. This acknowledgment of a pointed remark or reply comes from fencing, where it is the word exclaimed to acknowledge the opponent's hit (it is French for "touched"). Technically, a hit is contact made with the point (or edge if using a saber) on an opponent; it scores as a point only if made in the approved target area. It began to be used figuratively in the late 19th century.

track record
A record of achievement or performance. The term comes from horse racing, where it signifies the best time a horse has ever made at a particular track or over a given distance. It began to be used figuratively in the 1940's.

> "I don't generally like running. I believe in training by rising gently up and down from the bench."
> —SATCHEL PAIGE, quoted by George Plimpton, Out of My League (1961)

training, to be in
Preparing for something. The term comes from numerous sports where athletes prepare for competition by using various forms of conditioning and practice, special diets, and the like. It has been used figuratively, often in jocular fashion, since about 1900, as in "She's tried on at least forty gowns; she's in training for her debut."

> "Garfein turns out to be a triple threat man—a strong composer . . . a strong librettist . . . and a strong stage director."
> —RICHARD DYER, Boston Globe, Feb. 29, 1992

triple threat
Great skill in three areas. The term comes from football, where it is used for an offensive player who can run, pass, and kick well. So used since about 1920, the term was adopted in baseball as an unofficial title for a pitcher who in a single season posts 20 wins, 200 or more strikeouts, and maintains an earned run average below 3.00. Merv Rettenmund once said

of his teammate Don Baylor, who had a sore arm: "He is the guts of the Angels, our triple threat. He can hit, run, and lob."

"When Greeks joyn'd Greeks, then was the tug of war."

—NATHANIEL LEE, *The Rival Queen,* 4:2 (1677)

tug of war
A fierce fight for supremacy. Whether this term ever designated a military contest is no longer known, although the quotation above implies that it did. Since the 19th century, however, it has been a form of athletic contest in which two teams pull against each other on opposite ends of a rope, trying to pull the center of the rope over a mark on the ground. It has been transferred to other kinds of fierce struggle since the second half of the 19th century.

turning a hair, without
Unruffled and calm. The term comes from horse racing, where an extremely sweaty horse has roughened hair. Jane Austen referred to it in *Northanger Abbey* (1798): "Hot! He [the horse] had not turned a hair till we came to Walcot church" (cited by *OED*). The term began to be used figuratively, but only in the negative, in the late 19th century, as in "He accepted her abuse without turning a hair."

two strikes against: *see* STRIKE(S) AGAINST.

ugly customer
A difficult, hostile individual; one likely to make trouble. This term dates from the early 19th century. Because the *OED*'s earliest citation is from an 1811 issue of *Sporting Magazine*, it seems safe to speculate that it was first used for a belligerent spectator at some sporting event and therefore merits inclusion here. W. Willmot Dixon, who wrote under the pseudonym Thormanby, suggested it came from boxing (*Boxers and Their Battles*, 1900). Certainly ugly customers at athletic events still abound, particularly when feelings run high. At important European soccer matches in recent years, riots have been a commonplace, sometimes even causing deaths. However, the term has also been used figuratively for mean or vicious individuals since the 1840's (Dickens so used it in *Martin Chuzzlewit*).

unassisted: *see* ASSIST.

under the wire
Scarcely or barely; just within some limit. The term comes from horse racing, where the wire marked the finish line. It began to be used figuratively during the first half of the 20th century, as in "Sandy got her story in just under the wire." See also DOWN TO THE WIRE.

up, to be
To have one's turn, to be ready for. The term comes from baseball, where it signifies being the individual (or team) at bat. Indeed, the traditional umpire's cry at the beginning or resumption of play is "Batter up!" In the 20th century the expression began to be used figuratively, as in "Charles thought he was up for a promotion." Also see ON DECK.

upshot

Result or conclusion; also, the gist. The term comes from medieval archery, where it signified the last shot in a tournament. By 1600 it was being used figuratively, by Shakespeare among others, in the sense of end result. Somewhat later in the 1600's it also became a synonym for the gist of an argument—the outcome of its premises—as in "The upshot of my argument was simply this" (Richard Kerwan, *Geological Essays*, 1799; cited by *OED*). Today it tends to be used more in the meaning of final result.

up to scratch: *see* COME UP TO SCRATCH.

V V V V V

"*Volleyball is a dandy game, and more besides.*"
—PETER WARDALE, *Volleyball: Skill and Tactics* (1964)

volleyball diplomacy
The potential resumption of friendly relations between Cuba and the United States. The term was coined in 1971, when an American volleyball team competed in Cuba in an Olympic playoff series and reported that they received a cordial reception. It is a play on the contemporary PING-PONG diplomacy concerning the resumption of normal relations between the United States and mainland China.

W W W W W

Wait till next year

The losers' battle cry. The term gained currency in baseball, where it was long associated with the Brooklyn Dodgers. The Dodgers lost the World Series to the New York Yankees in 1941, 1947, 1949, 1952, 1953, and 1956, and after each loss allegedly greeted their long-time rivals with this expression. Jackie Robinson used it as the title of his 1960 autobiography.

> "Every artist walks a tightrope between intention and achievement."
>
> —JOHN PERCIVAL, *Experimental Dance* (1971)

walk a tightrope, to

To achieve a delicate balance. The term comes from gymnastics and acrobatics, and refers to the feat of performing on a tightly stretched rope or cable. It was being used figuratively by the early 20th century.

walkover, a

An easy victory or task. The term comes from racing, where it denotes the result when only a single contestant or horse is left in a race and must merely complete the course at any pace in order to be declared the winner. It has been used figuratively since the early 19th century.

In gymnastics, however, the word has another, quite different meaning. It is a stunt in which the gymnast, from a standing position, leans forward or backward, puts the hands on the floor, brings one leg at a time up over the head, pauses in handstand position, and brings the legs down one at a time to finish in a standing position. Needless to say, this kind of walkover is anything but a walkover.

"Most people think I'm practicing before I play, but I'm not. I'm just warming up. I practice after the round."

—Golfer JACK NICKLAUS, quoted by John
Madden, *Hey, Wait a Minute* (1984)

warm up, to
Also, *a warm-up*. To prepare for an event, by practicing or some other means. It is difficult to say in just which sport this term originated, since it is used in just about all of them and has been since the late 19th century. The verb has also been used as a noun since the early 20th century, and both forms have been transferred to other kinds of preparation since about 1940. For example, the *Baltimore Sun* referred to the bombing of several Pacific islands as "warmup attacks" (May 22, 1943).

In the second half of the 20th century, with increasing interest in jogging and other forms of exercise in the interests of general fitness (rather than athletic competition), the name *warmups*, for *warmup suit*, began to be used for sweat suits and similar attire worn for running in cold weather, warming up, or simply for looking fashionably athletic.

Way to go!
Exclamation of approval and encouragement. It appears to have originated among American coaches of athletic teams from about 1950 on, who used it to urge on athletes who were performing well. It gained more general currency on a popular American television show, Rowan and Martin's *Laugh-In*, in the 1960's, and continues to be used in a variety of situations calling for such approbation.

white hope
A person or object expected (or hoped) to achieve well in some sphere. The term originally was coined for a white boxer—any white boxer—who could defeat the seemingly invincible heavyweight champion, Jack Johnson, who was black. Johnson held the title from 1908 to 1915. The term gained fur-

ther currency when it was used as the title of a Broadway play based on Jack Johnson, *The Great White Hope*, and soon was used figuratively for anyone or anything of whom/which a great deal was anticipated.

whitewash

A victory in which the opposition scores nothing. The term originated in 19th-century baseball, and presumably referred to the blank score of the opposing team. In the late 20th century it was being used figuratively for similar victories in other areas, as in "Our high-school debaters are undefeated, and their last three were a whitewash." It is also used in verb form, *to whitewash.*

> *"This was something new to him, trackee instead of a tracker, and he wasn't sure he liked it. Whole new ball game, and with a whole new set of rules."*
> —TOM KAKONIS, *Double Down* (1991)

whole new ball game, a

A completely new start; an entirely different matter. The term comes from baseball, where it denotes a situation in which the game turns around fast, with the team that is behind forging ahead. In America the word *ball game* nearly always refers to baseball or softball, despite the fact that some form of ball is used in approximately eighty different games played throughout the world. They range in size from the 30-inch basketball to the 1.6-inch ball used in golf.

wide of the mark: *see* MISS THE MARK.

wild goose chase

A senseless pursuit; a hopeless enterprise. The term originally meant a kind of horse race popular in the 16th century, in which riders had to follow whoever was in the lead in a particular formation. It was probably so called because they resembled a flock of geese in flight. The term was already being transferred by Shakespeare's time, as in his "Nay, if our wits run the wild-goose chase, I am done" (*Romeo and Juliet*, 2:4).

wild pitch
A careless statement or action. The term comes from baseball, where it refers to a pitched ball so far off target that the catcher misses it and a base runner advances. It is then charged as an error to the pitcher. Dating from about 1880, the term began to be transferred to more general errors in the mid-20th century, as in "Calling Norman Mailer a true scholar—that's a wild pitch."

win hands down: *see* HANDS DOWN.

> "*I do not believe that the guy who said that winning is the most important thing was right, at least not in baseball, but winning covers up a great number of problems.*"
> —New York Yankees pitcher ALLIE REYNOLDS

"Winning isn't everything, it's the only thing"
The end is what counts, no matter what means are used to attain it. This bloodthirsty statement is usually attributed to Green Bay Packers football coach Vince Lombardi (1913–70), but Chicago White Sox president Bill Veeck has also been credited with it. Springing to Lombardi's defense, Howard Cosell maintained, "Winning, and above all, playing at your best level, were important to him, but that did not compromise his standards of honesty and fair play" (*What's Wrong with Sports*, 1991). The idea, of course, is hardly new. John Heywood's epigram collection of 1562 had, "He pleyth best that wins." But it is Lombardi's version that is most often heard today, not only in sports but in any competitive enterprise.

"Win (this) one for the Gipper"
A maudlin appeal to a group to do their best. This statement was allegedly first uttered by the legendary Notre Dame foot-

ball coach, Knute Rockne, in 1921. "The Gipper" was the nickname of his star player, George Gipp, who was terminally ill, and Rockne was giving his team a pep talk, exhorting them to win an upcoming game for the sake of their dying teammate. He probably repeated it more than once. It gained further currency through a motion picture about Rockne, *Knute Rockne, All American* (1940), in which Pat O'Brien played the coach and Ronald Reagan, playing Gipp, was the one who uttered the famous lines. Decades later, when Reagan was President, he was sometimes mockingly referred to as the Gipper. Today the expression is nearly always used ironically.

win on points, to
To succeed, but just barely. The term comes from boxing, where in the absence of a knockout the winner is decided on the basis of points awarded for each round. The term was transferred to figurative use in the second half of the 20th century.

"What's lost today may be won tomorrow."
—MIGUEL DE CERVANTES, *Don Quixote* (1605)

win some, lose some, (you can)
The fatalistic response of a loser. The expression is thought to have originated in the early 20th century among gamblers on baseball and other sports events (there is a variant, *win some, lose some, some rained out,* that suggests baseball as the origin). It was being used figuratively by the 1940's, as in Charles Williams's novel, *And the Deep Blue Sea*: "She stopped . . . and shrugged. You won a few, you lost a few." See also YOU CAN'T WIN 'EM ALL.

wipeout
A decisive defeat. This meaning of "wipeout" comes from sports, where it designates an overwhelming victory by one side. Possibly from this usage the word came to be used in surfing for a very serious fall, in which the surfer is in danger of being struck by the board and/or of being driven into the

rough ocean bottom by surf. "Wipeout" is used similarly in skiing, cycling, and motorcycle racing, for a dangerous fall.

wipe the floor: *see* MOP UP THE FLOOR.

with the gloves off: *see* BARE-KNUCKLE.

workout
A practice session or test. The term originated in boxing about 1900 for a practice bout, and was soon taken over with similar meanings in such sports as track and football. It also acquired the meaning of a training session, especially a structured regime of exercise, a usage that persists, as in "David goes to the gym for a workout three times a week." (It also appears in verb form, *to work out*, meaning to engage in structured exercise.) From the sports meanings have come more figurative ones, as in "I'm doing my own tax returns and giving my adding machine a good workout."

World Series
A major championship. The term comes from baseball's World Series, a post-season playoff played annually as a best-of-seven games series between the pennant winners of the two major leagues, the National and the American. The first World Series took place in 1903, and since then the only year skipped has been 1904. From the 1930's to the late 1950's the New York Yankees dominated World Series play, winning seventeen times between 1932 and 1958. In the late 20th century other competitions, ranging from bicycle races to golf matches and television quiz shows, have adopted the name World Series, which nevertheless remains as closely associated with baseball as the World Cup is with soccer.

"He that is thrown would ever wrestle."

—THOMAS FULLER, *Gnomologia* (1732)

wrestle to the ground, to

To overcome with considerable effort. The word "wrestle" has since the year 1000 denoted the physical struggle entailed in this sport. By the 12th century it was being used figuratively for nonphysical struggles of various kinds.

Wrestling, the sport in which two unarmed individuals attempt to subdue each other, is believed to be some 5,000 years old. The modern sport of wrestling has two principal forms, freestyle and Greco-Roman, differing mainly in the kinds of hold permitted. In both the opponents try to throw each other to the mat and secure holds that score points or enable them to pin the opponent's back or shoulders to the mat for a given time. Professional wrestling, which is conducted more as an entertainment than a sport, relies on showmanship for its appeal. An individual wins when the opponent is pinned or withdraws.

The phrase here, which is a more graphic one than the older *to wrestle down,* has been around since at least the 19th century. Massachusetts Governor William Weld used it in his first state-of-the-state speech (Jan. 16, 1992), saying the administration's principal task would be to wrestle the state's budget to the ground.

XYZ XYZ XYZ

"Any club that would accept me as a member, I wouldn't want to join."

—Attributed to GROUCHO MARX

yacht club

A symbol of high social status. Literally, it denotes an organization for encouraging and directing the sport of yachting. In practice yachting is a very costly sport. Although today many yacht clubs provide berths for sailboats much less grand than a yacht, in some clubs membership is still very expensive, if not restricted on other grounds, and so the association with upper-class snobbery remains attached to the term.

The major yachting competition is the America's Cup, which grew out of the first contest to establish a world yachting championship in 1851. This race, open to all classes of yacht from all over the world, covered a 60-mile course around the Isle of Wight. The prize was a cup worth about $500, which was donated by the Royal Yacht Squadron of England. It came to be called the America's Cup because the first winner was the United States yacht *America*. U.S. yachtsmen continued to win the cup, despite efforts by mainly British and Australian opponents, until 1983, when the Australian yacht *Australia II* defeated the U.S. entry *Liberty*. Tom Callahan later commented on this loss, "Only a few millionaires with wet bottoms were very disappointed" (*Time*, Feb. 9, 1987). And sportswriter Ira Berkow of the *New York Times* wrote about the 1987 race, "If millionaires and corporations want to spend their money trying to drown one another in the Indian Ocean—the movers and shakers are still millionaires and corporations at that level—then who am I to try to stop them" (Feb. 10, 1987).

"So remarkable is his memory that he has virtually total recollection of each encounter. 'You can look it up,' he'll say to doubters. They do and doubt no longer."
—New York Times profile of CASEY STENGEL, Oct. 19, 1960

"You can/could look it up"

I am giving you the true facts. This particular statement was often made by long-time Yankees manager Casey Stengel (1890–1975), who managed his team to ten pennants and seven championships between 1949 and 1960, an unequaled record. After the 1960 season he was fired because of his advanced age, but a year later he was hired as manager of the new National League team, the New York Mets. Known as much for his dicta and innumerable anecdotes as for his managing skill, Stengel earned the nickname the "Old Perfesser." His oft-repeated assertion of his own accurate memory was used by numerous other baseball figures, notably Leo Durocher and Jim Bouton. James Thurber used the expression as the title of a 1941 short story, a tall tale told by an old-time trainer who is sure of his facts but very hazy about dates and, while reminiscing, keeps repeating "You could look it up."

"You can't win all of the time. There are guys out there who are better than you."
—Attributed to YOGI BERRA

You can't win 'em all

A loser's deprecatory understatement after suffering a severe defeat. The statement undoubtedly comes from sports, but its true origin is anyone's guess. Nevertheless, it is associated with Boston pitcher Clifton G. Curtis, who made it after losing the twenty-third consecutive game in the 1910–11 season. It was also repeated by long-time Philadelphia Athletics manager Connie Mack after losing a total of 117 games in 1916. During his half-century tenure the Athletics won the pennant nine times and the World Series five times. See also WIN SOME, LOSE SOME.

zone defense

Protecting a particular area or field. The term comes from such team sports as football and basketball, where it denotes assigning each defensive player to a specific portion of the playing area, where he guards only those opponents who enter that zone. It is in direct contrast to man-to-man defense, in which a defensive player guards a particular opponent on all portions of the playing area (also see ONE-ON-ONE). In the late 20th century the term occasionally began to be used figuratively, as in "Our salesmen are concentrating on zone defense, rather than taking on any individual competitors."

INDEX

In this index, all cross-references refer to main entries in the body of the book, which are listed alphabetically. For example, the index entry "zone, the: *see* END ZONE" directs the reader to look up the entry **end zone** in the book, on page 61. In some cases very long entry names may be abbreviated in the index; thus, "can't hit the broad side of a barn" may be shortened to "can't hit the broad side."

As in the body of the book, entries in the index are listed alphabetically, letter by letter up to the comma in the case of inversion, and numerals are alphabetized as though they were written out (.400 is alphabetized as "four hundred").

"Winning isn't everything, it's the
only thing" 241
"Win (this) one for the Gipper"
241–42
win on points, to 242
win some, lose some (you can)
242
wipeout 242–43
wipe the floor: see MOP/WIPE THE
FLOOR WITH, TO
with the gloves off: see BARE-
KNUCKLE
workout 243
World Golf Hall of Fame 146
World Series 243

wrestle down: see WRESTLE TO THE
GROUND
wrestle to the ground, to 244–45

XYZ

yacht club 246
Yastremski, Carl 170
"You can/could look it up" 247
you can run but can't hide: see RUN
BUT CAN'T . . .
You can't win 'em all 247
zone, the: see under END ZONE
zone defense 248